Owen C Whitehouse

A Primer of Hebrew Antiquities

Owen C Whitehouse

A Primer of Hebrew Antiquities

ISBN/EAN: 9783337316198

Printed in Europe, USA, Canada, Australia, Japan

Cover: Foto ©ninafisch / pixelio.de

More available books at **www.hansebooks.com**

Present Day Primers

A PRIMER OF HEBREW ANTIQUITIES

BY

OWEN C. WHITEHOUSE, M.A.

Principal and Professor of Hebrew, Cheshunt College

London
THE RELIGIOUS TRACT SOCIETY
56, PATERNOSTER ROW; AND 65, ST. PAUL'S CHURCHYARD
1895

TABLE OF CONTENTS

INTRODUCTION

                                                  PAGE

1. Definition of the subject and general principles . . 7

CHAPTER I
THE FAMILY AND HOUSEHOLD OCCUPATIONS

2. The Hebrew family.—Father, mother.—Marriage . 10
3. Marriage customs, wedding ceremonies . . . 14
4. Position of the wife.—Divorce 17
5. Children. — Circumcision. — Naming. — Weaning. — Parental relation and responsibility. . . . 20
6. Inheritance.—Ownership of property by women.—Primogeniture 23
7. Slaves and slavery.—Position and rights of slaves.—Price of slaves.—Ameliorating conditions.—Year of release.—Female slaves 28
8. Clothing.—Materials employed.—Different articles of attire for both sexes.—Ornaments of women.—Sandals—Jewellery. 40
9. Dwellings: caves, tents, houses.—Materials employed.—Interior adornment 57
10. Pleasure-gardens. 65
11. Household furniture. — Handmill, kneading trough, and oven 67
12. Kitchen utensils, pots, pitchers, bottles, and baskets . 75

CHAPTER II
OUT-DOOR LIFE AND OCCUPATIONS

13. Pastoral life.—Dress and accoutrements of the shepherd.—Sheep.—Goats 78
14. Canaanite civilization and its influence on Israel.—

		PAGE
	Agriculture.—Ox, ass, mule, and horse, and their employment	82
15.	Climate of Palestine.—Early and latter rain.—Agricultural implements: plough, ox goad. — Sowing: barley and wheat-harvest.—Reaping.—Threshing.—Winnowing	84
16.	Vine-culture and vintage.—Wine-press and wine-vat.—Feast of Booths.—Raisins.—Drinking habits.—Intemperance	95
17.	Olive and its culture.—Olive-oil and its uses . .	104
18.	Fig and its culture.—Varieties.—Its uses.—Date-palm. Sycamore.— Pomegranate.—Cereals (millet spelt, etc.).—Beans.—Lentils.—Cucumbers.—Flax .	110
19.	Handicrafts and their development.—Pottery.—Influence of Egypt and Babylonia.—Potter's-wheel	113
20.	Weaving.—Looms	119
21.	Workmanship in wood, stone, and metal.—Influence of Phœnicia.—Bronze and iron age.—Canaanite arts adopted by the Hebrews.—Smelting and forging.—Manufacture of idols.—Names of tools . . .	120
22.	Writing, Hieroglyphic, Cuneiform and Phœnician.—Writing materials and instruments.—Scribes .	126
23.	Seals.—Documents	132
24.	Trade.—Phœnician vessels.—'Ships of Tarshish.'—Naval ports.—Trade quarters	134
25.	Etiquette and social intercourse.—Salutations.—Buying and selling.—Gate of the city.—Hospitality.—Meals and banquets	137
26.	Death and funeral customs.—Graves . . .	144

CHAPTER III

SOCIAL AND POLITICAL ORGANIZATION

27.	Family clan and tribe.—Judge and elders.—King.—State officials.—Royal prerogative and its abuse.—Revenues.—High Priest in post-exilian times.—Sanhedrin	147

APPENDICES

A. Money: B. Weights: C. Measures of capacity and length: D. Calendar: E. Sacrifices . . .		154

HEBREW ANTIQUITIES

INTRODUCTION

1. **Definition.** By the 'Antiquities' of the Old Testament two different classes of subjects are meant. The term includes, *first*, the *material objects* of human life, such as dwellings and clothing; also the implements, agricultural, martial, political, and even religious, which find mention in the Old Testament, and whereby human life under the ancient Hebrew civilization, in its varied relations, was maintained, and its usages carried on. And it includes, *secondly*, the *usages* themselves, the employments, the organized *institutions* and laws, whether social or religious, belonging to the Hebrew society or state described in the Old Testament.

As this subject in its varied branches is very extensive, it will be impossible, within the limits of this work, to deal with every topic that a larger treatise might be expected to include. The most important only can be here referred to, and these cannot be described with the fulness which a complete dictionary of antiquities might bestow. We shall endeavour, however, to set forth the salient features with as much vividness and truth as possible. With a view to accuracy of delineation it will be necessary for the reader to be reminded that all earthly human institutions *grow*. And the institutions of Israel, whether religious or political, constituted no exception to this universal law. They were not the same in the days of the Judges as they were in the time of Jeremiah. So far as the date of the Old Testament documents will enable us, we shall endeavour to present our subjects in their historical development. Owing to lack of space the subject of *religious institutions* can only be referred to incidentally.

Furthermore, it is important to recognise that the Israelites did not stand entirely alone among the peoples of the world. For it is quite certain that the usages which prevailed among them and the language which they spoke were nearly identical with those of the other races, such as the Canaanites and the Moabites, which dwelt near them. The Hebrews exhibited many features of closest resemblance to other races which in common with them are called Semitic, viz., the Arabs of the South, the Aramæans or Syrians of the North, and the Assyrians and Babylonians on the East. Modern archæology is continually demonstrating this with increasing clearness, and we shall make use of some of its results in throwing all the light we can upon the antiquities of Israel.

The ancient Hebrews, therefore, grew up among kindred Semitic peoples. Not only their language but the material objects and instruments and the primitive usages of their civilization were derived from a common stock of ancient Semitic inheritance, much of which the Semites again shared with the other ancient races of the world. What then made the ancient Hebrews distinctive among the races of the earth as God's own 'peculiar' people? Not so much the religious institutions which grew up among them, and also among the kindred races, and were derived from an immemorial antiquity, as those higher ideas which in the course of Divine teaching awoke to life and energy, and which their religious institutions became moulded to enshrine and express.

The period of time covered in this brief treatise will be about a thousand years, viz., from the Exodus, circ. 1300 B.C., to 300 B.C. After the latter date Jewish institutions became to a certain extent moulded by Greek civilization and ideas—slowly, it is true, and amid some resistance from the conservative Pharisaic party, yet also surely and inevitably. Occasional reference only will be made to the literature of the Apocrypha, the New Testament, and of the latest Old Testament documents.

CHAPTER I

THE FAMILY AND HOUSEHOLD OCCUPATIONS

The Hebrew Family. The position of the father of the family in primitive Israel was evidently that of an absolute ruler, though custom tended to make his rule milder than it otherwise would have been. The very name for husband in Hebrew, *ba'al*, possessor or lord, is a clear indication of what has been said. His wife was regarded as his property; and since polygamy was universally prevalent, and dissolution of the marriage relationship might take place at the will of the husband, her relation to the husband was rendered thereby one of subordination and dependence.

To a man of full-grown age continuance in the unmarried state was regarded in the East as very unusual.[1] This was due to the universal desire of every man and woman for posterity, especially male posterity. Whether this was connected with the ancient worship of ancestors by the family[2] need not

---

[1] 'To abstain from marrying when a man has attained a sufficient age, and when there is no impediment, is esteemed by the Egyptians improper and even disreputable.'—LANE, *Modern Egyptians*.

[2] The *Teraphim* were ancestral images. That they much resembled the human form may be inferred from Michal's device (1 Sam. xix. 13). Neubauer traces an etymological connection between this word and the word *Rephaim*, or spirits of the departed in Sheol or Hades. The episode described in Genesis

be discussed here. It is at all events certain that the ancient Israelite considered that his name and personality were in some way perpetuated by the continued existence of his descendants. Thus sterility was regarded by a woman as the most terrible misfortune (Gen. xvi. 2; 1 Sam. i. 2-8), while loss of children or the destruction of a family were looked upon as signs of Divine wrath (1 Kings xvi. 34; Deut. xxviii. 56, 57). Hence, on a daughter's departure from her parents' dwelling for her husband's home, the highest parting blessing was the wish that she might become mother of thousands (Gen. xxiv. 60; comp. Ps. xlv. 16, 17). No more distinguishing token of Divine favour could be imagined by an ancient Hebrew than abundance of posterity (Gen. xiii. 16, xv. 5, etc.; Deut. xxxiii. 24).

Early marriages are the rule among Orientals in the present day. Indeed, Lane assures us that few women in Egypt remain unmarried after the age of sixteen, and marriages at the age of twelve or thirteen are quite common. Probably in ancient Israel it was much the same. Under these circumstances marriage comes largely under the control of the parents on both sides. Of this we have a vivid illustration in the detailed narrative contained in Genesis xxiv. From this account we see that Abraham gave special orders to his servant to seek out a wife for Isaac. The father plays a prominent part in all the preliminary arrangements, and the whole matter is determined by his instructions. The part played by Isaac is quite subordinate. Similarly, in Judges xiv. 1-4, the parents of Samson endeavour

xxxi. 19, 32-35 would suggest that the Teraphim corresponded to the Roman *lares*.

though unsuccessfully, to control their son's choice, and they accompany him to the bride's abode in Timnath, to settle the preliminaries.

Another important point still characteristic of Oriental life, namely, the tendency to keep the marriage in the same kindred or clan, emerges from the narrative in Genesis xxiv. Marriage with another race was strongly deprecated, as this meant the abandonment of national *sacra*, and in comparatively early times express *Tôrôth*, or instructions, whether oral or written, were in existence on this subject (Exod. xxxiv. 15, 16 ;[1] comp. the more definite prescription, Deut. vii. 3, 4). That such marriages, though deprecated,

[1] It is to be noted that the religious tie fell more lightly on the men than on the women. The *sacra* of the wife's tribe (Exod. xxxiv. 16) draw away the husband and his children, not *vice versâ*. Comp. Gen. xxxi. 32, foll.; 1 Kings xi. 4. The tendency was precisely the opposite in Roman law, in which the wife abandoned her previous *gens* and its *sacra* for those of her husband. In fact, Exodus xxxiv. 16 suggests the question whether the primitive custom of *beena*, as opposed to *baal* marriage may not in very early times have prevailed even in Canaan. By *beena* marriages are meant those 'unions in which the husband goes to settle in his wife's village' or is received by the woman in her own tent. Kinship will then be reckoned on the mother's side, the children being reared under the protection of the mother's kin. *Baal* marriage, which prevailed among the Hebrews, and in later times among the Arabs, inverts this relation. The husband is the lord or owner (*ba'al*). The wife follows the husband, and the children are regarded as belonging to his kin. This interesting subject is worked out with great mastery of detail in Robertson Smith's *Kinship and Marriage in Early Arabia.* This writer thinks that Genesis ii. 24 and the name of Eve point to primitive *beena* traditions and female kinship even among the Hebrews (comp. Arabic *chayy*, which means female kinship or tribe). Judges xiv. 10-20 indicates an approximation to this custom. It is quite evident that the prevalence of *baal* marriage tended to convert the position of the woman from a relation of independence into one of subservience. It is possible that a struggle between these two traditions underlies the narrative Gen. xxxi.

did take place, is evident from the example of Samson (Judg. xiv. 3; comp. also Gen. xxxiv., Ruth i. 4). These, of course, were departures from ordinary usage.

Intertribal marriage, however, within the same race was by no means uncommon. The special prohibition enforced against the tribe of Benjamin in Judges xxi. 7 is described as exceptional, and arising from an exceptional cause. The prevalent custom appears to have been to take a wife from the *agnati* or kindred on the father's side. Obviously the ancient Hebrew felt preference rather than aversion to cousin marriage. Nay, a half-sister, provided the relationship was paternal, might without any obstacle be chosen for a bride, as we know from the example of Abraham and Sarah (comp. 2 Sam. xiii. 13; 1 Kings xv. 2, which show that such unions were sanctioned in the time of David and Solomon); and from the inscription of the Phœnician king of Sidon, Eshmunazar, lines 14, 15, we learn that he was son of Tabnith and his half-sister Em'astoreth, priestess of Ashtoreth. Such unions took place among the Persians, Greeks, and Egyptians, but were forbidden in Deuteronomy xxvii. 22, Leviticus xviii. 9, xx. 17. Yet such marriages were probably not by any means so common as those with cousins upon the father's side. Cousin marriage is at the present day 'very common among the Arabs of Egypt and of other countries' (Lane). Thus in the Old Testament we read that Abraham despatched his servant Eleazer to Mesopotamia to secure a cousin, Rebekah, for his son Isaac, and similarly Jacob marries his cousins Leah and Rachel.[1]

[1] 'Amongst the Bedouin a man has the right to demand his

3. **Marriage Customs.** We have already stated that the Hebrews and Canaanites regarded the husband as the *baʻal*, 'owner' or lord of the wife. This in all probability arose from a primitive condition of warfare, in which the husband captured the wife. That wives were not infrequently obtained in this way in Old Testament times is obvious from the law respecting the captive wife in Deuteronomy xxi. 10 foll. For capture the more peaceful method of purchase became substituted when human life grew more civilized. The price—paid frequently in flocks or camels, sometimes in money—was called *mōhar* (Arabic *mahr*). From Exodus xxii. 16, illustrated by the more expanded form of the statute in Deuteronomy xxii. 29, we learn that the *mōhar* or purchase money for a bride was usually fifty shekels (between six and seven pounds sterling). It was also customary for the bridegroom at this preliminary stage, through his representative, to make a gift to the bride of jewels and raiment (Gen. xxiv. 22, 53). According to Lane, this is done after the conclusion of the marriage contract and previous to the wedding, among modern Arabs. 'He sends to her two or three or more times some fruit, sweetmeats, etc., and perhaps makes her a present of a shawl, or some other article of value.' In conducting the preliminaries, the father, or, if he be dead, the elder brother of the future bride, plays the chief part, as being her natural protector. The bride herself in these earlier stages is prevented by etiquette from taking any but a purely passive part in the proceedings. In Isaiah iv. 1 the depopulation

cousin in marriage, and she cannot refuse him.'—LAYARD, *Nineveh and Babylon*, abridged ed., p. 135 footnote.

of the country, the destruction of males, and the consequent position of the women, are described as so terrible that maidens are driven to sue for their own marriage. It has been already stated that the bridegroom also took no prominent share in the preliminary negotiations, which were settled by the parents. In Syria, and perhaps some parts of Palestine, the custom prevailed in ancient times of giving the elder sister first in marriage (Genesis xxix. 26). According to Lane, this tradition is still preserved among the Arabs.

The wedding ceremonies began with a feast at the dwelling of the bride. This we infer to have been the custom in the earlier period described in Genesis xxiv. and Judges xiv.[1] In the case of Samson's wedding festivities at Timnath, the residence of his bride, we are told that it was Samson who made the feast, and that this was the custom of those early times ('for so used the young men to do'). Samson was joined by thirty companions of his wife's kindred, and the festivities lasted an entire week, and were enlivened by riddles. In the ancient Semitic, as well as Greek and Roman custom, the chief and most significant part of all the ceremonies was the escorting of the bride in festive procession to her future

---

[1] In later times the feast was held in the house of the bridegroom, as described in Lane's *Modern Egyptians*, and this form of marriage custom evidently underlies our Lord's parable (Matt. xxv. 1–13). The virgins were waiting till the bridegroom should appear to escort the bridal party to the feast in his own house. Meyer, it is true, interprets the facts otherwise, but the position of the bridegroom in John ii. 9, 10, to whom the governor of the feast appeals, is decisive in favour of the view here advocated, and it is fully sustained by Tobit vii. 13, xi. 17–19. See also Dr. Edersheim's *Life and Times of the Messiah*, vol. i. pp. 354, 355.

husband's home with songs and rejoicings that became proverbial of a nation's ordinary prosperity (Jer. vii. 34, xvi. 9, xxv. 10). The splendour of the dresses and other accompaniments would, of course, vary with the wealth of the families in which the union took place. From Isaiah lxi. 10 we learn that the bridegroom wore an elegant turban, while the bride was decked with jewels. The latter also enveloped her body in a light shawl or veil (*ts'àiph*). The same custom prevails at the present day, as we learn from Lane's *Modern Egyptians*. Nor must we forget the girdle of which Jeremiah (ii. 20) makes special mention. The bride was accompanied by maidens, and in the case of a royal marriage the splendour of her robes and the pomp of the procession may be best described in the language of the royal epithalamium, Psalm xlv. 14–16 (Heb. 13 foll.).

'And, O Tyrian maid,[1] with a present there do homage to
   thee
The rich among the people!
All splendour is the king's daughter within doors,
Of gold broidery her garment;
In robes of gay colours she is conducted to the king,
Maidens behind her, her companions, are brought unto thee;
They are conducted with gladness and exultation,
They enter into the palace of the king.'

---

[1] The text is by no means certain. We have simply followed the Massoretic. The occurrence of a vocative here is somewhat questionable. Dr. Edersheim's vivid description of the escorting of the bride to her husband's home may here be quoted:—'First came the merry sounds of music, then they who distributed among the people wine and oil, and nuts among the children; next the bride, covered with the bridal veil, her long hair flowing, surrounded by her companions, and led by the friends of the bridegroom and children of the bride-chamber. Some carried torches or lamps on poles; those nearest had myrtle branches and chaplets of flowers.'

Lastly, she was escorted to the bridal chamber, or, properly speaking, a pavilion, which was curtained off, the Hebrew name for which was *Chuppah*,[1] where stood the *'eres*, or nuptial couch.

4. The position of the **wife** in a Hebrew household suffered from the prevalence of polygamy; and since, as we have shown above, marriage was based on the idea of wife purchase by the husband, who was her lord and owner, it follows that a husband could take to himself as many wives as he pleased, the number being limited solely by his means of support, or his personal inclination. As a matter of fact, the wealthier the individual the larger as a rule became the number. Moreover, there existed certain causes which tended to bring about polygamy. In the first place, as Stade points out, the wife was married so young that she was unequal to the duties which fell upon her as mistress of the household, and needed the assistance of others. In the second place, it happened sometimes that, owing to the wife's childlessness, esteemed by Orientals a calamity— almost a curse—another consort would frequently be sought in order that posterity—so much longed for— might be obtained. Childlessness, indeed, came as a sad blight and dishonour upon a woman in her lord's household, and she esteemed it as such. Under these circumstances she would often induce her husband to accept a concubine of her own choice, and inferior to her in social position—in fact, her female slave, whose offspring she would regard as her own (Gen. xvi. 2, xxx. 3, 9). Childbearing, therefore,

---

[1] See Cheyne, *Book of Psalms*, on Ps. xix. 5, and Robertson Smith, *Kinship and Marriage*, p. 168.

conferred dignity and importance on the wife. It is easy to see that out of these conditions of polygamic life heart-burnings and jealousies were sure to arise.

A man had the power at will to cancel the marriage bond. Not so, however, the wife. But the woman under these circumstances possessed certain rights. The primitive code of legislation usually called the 'Book of the Covenant' (Exod. xx. 22-xxiii.) evidently shows that this was the case, even when she was in the position of a bondwoman sold by the parents into concubinage. If she ceased to please her master, he had no right to sell her like a chattel to foreigners. He might indeed under such circumstances espouse her to his son, in which case she was to be treated like one of his own daughters. Unless she were redeemed by her own kindred—in which condition she was free to marry another—he was obliged to continue to her food and raiment (Exod. xxi. 7-11). According to Burckhardt, among the higher classes in Arabia it is regarded as a shameful thing to sell a concubine. She remains all her life with her master. In very early times, however, it sometimes happened that the woman was simply dismissed from the master's home, as we see in the hard case of Hagar (Gen. xxi. 10 foll.). The master would then have no further rights, and gave up all claim to compensation if she married another.

As Hebrew society developed and became more civilized, it became more humanized, and numerous traits in the Deuteronomic legislation, which in its present form may be as late as the seventh century B.C., are clear indications of this social progress. Thus, according to Deuteronomy xv. 17, the female slave might, if she chose, claim the same right of freedom from her master at the end of seven years as a male slave.

We may regard in this light the *writ of divorce* prescribed in Deuteronomy xxiv. 1–4, and which the husband was bound to give into the hand of the wife whom he for special reasons dismissed from marriage relationship. This regulation, as Ewald shows (*Alterthümer*, p. 272), existed for the benefit of the wife, who was now definitely released from all claims on the part of a former husband and was free to marry another. At the same time it is clear that the Deuteronomic legislation aimed at greater strictness in the married relation, so as to correct those lax practices at which the higher moral consciousness of Israel revolted (Amos ii. 7; Ezek. xxii. 10). In earlier times, as among the Arabs, the father's wives (with the exception of the mother) came into the son's possession with the rest of the property. This we observe in the case of Absalom[1] (see 2 Sam. xvi. 22; comp. 2 Sam. iii. 7).

The lot of a wife who came from a wealthy or influential family would naturally be far more favourable than that of her less fortunate companions. A woman in such a position would bring property with her, which she had the right to own apart from her husband. Thus Hagar is recognised by Abraham as the slave of his wife Sarah, and the latter had absolute right to dispose of her bondmaid as she pleased (Gen. xvi. 6; comp. 1 Sam. xxv. 42). That the position of a wife in a wealthy Hebrew

---

[1] Robertson Smith, *Kinship and Marriage*, p. 89, and *Zeitschrift für die Alttestamentliche Wissenschaft*, 1892, p. 163.

household became in later times a very honourable one is clearly shown in the beautiful panegyric of a virtuous wife in Proverbs xxxi. 10 foll. (comp. xii. 4), and by the recognition of her moral influence and instruction conjointly with that of the husband in the training of the children (Exod. xx. 12; Deut. v. 16; Prov. i. 8, vi. 20, etc.). It is evident that even in early pre-exilian times far more freedom of intercourse was permitted to a Hebrew woman, whether married or unmarried, than prevails in modern Islam. Rebekah moves about freely with face unveiled until she approaches Isaac (Gen. xxiv. 64, 65). We read of the maidens of Shiloh dancing in the vineyards at the annual festival (Judg. xxi. 21), and women sing triumphal songs to greet Saul and David on their return (1 Sam. xviii. 6, 7). Women even became prophets like Huldah, and held the office of judge like Deborah (Judg. v.), or exercised active regal administration like Jezebel (1 Kings xviii. 13) or Athaliah (2 Kings xi. 3), and were treated with greatest deference like Bathsheba (1 Kings ii. 19).

5. **The children. Circumcision. Naming.** Childbirth entailed rites of purification, and the mother was compelled to absent herself from the sanctuary for thirty-three days in the case of a boy's birth, and for twice that period if the infant were a girl. After this period the Levitical law (Lev. xii. 6) prescribed that she should come to the sanctuary with an offering for her purification at the hands of the priest. The offering consisted of a lamb of the first year for a burnt-offering, and a young pigeon or turtle dove as a sin-offering.[1] On the eighth day

---

[1] According to Ezekiel xvi. 4 the newly-born child was not

the child, if a male, was *circumcised*. This rite of circumcision goes back into a hoary past, and was part of the common inheritance of the Hebrew and Canaanite, among other nations of antiquity. It was probably of *African* origin, and served to mark racial distinction (Stade). We learn from Herodotus (ii. 104), who wrote in the fifth century B.C., that both the Egyptians and Ethiopians circumcised their children in early infancy, and so also the Phœnicians and Syrians, who 'declared that they had learned the custom from the Egyptians.' This last statement must be accepted with caution. Prof. Sayce, however, has pointed out that a representation of the operation is to be found on the walls of the temple of Khonsu at Karnak. Mummies also show that the statement of Herodotus is quite correct, as far as the Egyptians are concerned. Among Mohammedan peoples of the present day it is performed on the child at the age of five or six, while 'among the peasants not infrequently at the age of twelve, thirteen, or fourteen' (Lane). The statement quoted above from Herodotus is supported by the statements of the Bible respecting the populations of Palestine, with the sole and remarkable exception of the Philistines, who are expressly spoken of as uncircumcised (1 Samuel *passim*). That the Canaanite tribes practised it may be inferred from the story of the Shechemites in Genesis xxxiv. Moreover Jeremiah

---

only washed in water but also rubbed over with salt. This use of *salt* may have been founded on certain hygienic properties, or on definite ritual traditions, such as the 'covenant of salt,' to which there is reference in Leviticus ii. 13, Numbers xviii. 19. It is well known that the eating of bread and salt constitutes a tie of brotherhood or friendship among the Arabs.

ix. 25, 26 (25 Heb.) obviously implies that circumcision prevailed not only in Egypt but also in Ammon, Edom, and Moab, which are classed with Judah in this respect.

This custom of circumcision belongs to a whole cycle of acts of self-offering. To the same class belong the offerings of hair and shaving of the head, whether as a vow or as a tribute to the dead. The wide prevalence of the latter custom is testified to in the Old Testament itself (Jer. ix. 26 (Heb. 25), which contained legislative prohibitions against those acts and against self-mutilation (Deut. xiv. 1; Levit. xix. 27). Circumcision is considered by Robertson Smith to have been originally 'a preliminary to marriage, and so a ceremony of introduction to the full prerogative of manhood.'[1] But when adopted into the Judaic system it became in course of time regarded as a sign that the child had entered into the covenant relations to Jehovah, and so an heir of the Divine promises (comp. Rom. iv. 11).

From numerous examples in Genesis we may infer that the *naming* of the child took place soon after birth, that the name was conferred by the mother, and was founded upon some event or domestic situation which was at the moment happening. As a matter of fact, however, the larger number of Hebrew and Canaanite proper names have a religious character and contain the names of Deity. See the Assyrian and Hebrew parallels which I have collated in Schrader's *Cuneiform Inscriptions and the Old Testament*, vol. ii. pp. 325 foll.; comp. Sayce's *Social Life among the Assyrians and Babylonians*, p. 52.

---

[1] *Religion of the Semites*, p. 310.

Occasionally the father re-named the child (Gen. xxxv. 18); indeed, a second name was by no means uncommon (*ibid.*, verse 10), as we know from the case of Saul of Tarsus and from instances in the Old Testament. Thus from 2 Samuel xxi. 19 it seems probable that El-Chanan was another name for David. We now know from the Babylonian documents that Pul and Tiglath Pileser were two names for the same person.

Hebrew children were not weaned till a year or two had elapsed, and when this took place it was celebrated by a family feast (Gen. xxi. 8; 1 Sam i. 21-24; comp. 2 Macc. vii. 27).

The relation of children to parents in a Hebrew household was one of subjection to authority. Death penalty was affixed for striking or reviling parents (Exod. xxi. 15-17). This principle of home life and family relationship, which is specially enforced in the Decalogue as the essential condition of prosperous social existence, and reiterated in the proverbs that prevail among the Jews (Prov. xix. 26, xx. 20, etc.), is beautifully exemplified in the life of our Lord, who though 'He advanced in wisdom and stature' was also 'subject to His parents' in the home at Nazareth. On the other hand, the duty of parents towards the children of instructing them in the ancestral traditions of their nation is recognised in the Deuteronomic legislation (Deut. vi. 6, 7, 20 foll., xi. 19, xxxi. 12, 13), as well as in the proverbs that became current among the people (Prov. xxii. 6, and i.-vii. *passim*, xv. 5).

6. As in ancient Greece and Rome, so in Israel, the custom of *inheritance* was that it should follow

the line of descent on the *father's* side (*agnati*). We hear of no example in the pre-exilian period of Israel's history of daughters sharing the inheritance with sons. The example to the contrary in Job xlii. 15 points, in the opinion of some scholars (*e.g.* Stade), to a post-exilian period.[1] Genesis xxi. 10, xxxi. 14 foll., and other passages prove that according to ancient Hebrew custom only the *sons* were qualified to inherit, and of these, moreover, only the sons of the wives recognised as such possessed *bonâ fide* rights (Gen. xxi. 10 foll., xxiv. 36, xxv. 5 foll.; Gen. xxi. 10 indicates, however, that the son of a concubine *could* inherit with other sons). This was probably connected with the fact that it was the son or heir to the father's property on whom the duty fell of perpetuating the family *sacra*—more especially the worship of the *Teraphim*, to which reference has already been made (see footnote, p. 10). This, as Stade has shown,[2] was in all probability the dominating factor in these arrangements. As we learn from Genesis xv. 2 foll., in default of sons by the free-born wives the son of a bondmaid would in the last resort inherit the father's wealth and perpetuate the family *sacra*. This, however, was but the exception that confirms the rule, well illustrated in the case of Jephthah, son of Gilead, related in Judges xi. 2. If the father had daughters only, and no male issue, the daughters were allowed to inherit, as we learn from the case of the daughters

---

[1] But the assignment of a field with springs to Achsah by her father Caleb in Joshua xv. 18, 19, should make us pause to acccept this argument as conclusive.

[2] *Geschichte des Volkes Israel*, p. 391. The writer takes this opportunity of expressing his obligations to this deeply interesting and masterly work.

of Zelophehad, narrated in Numbers xxvii. 1–11. Whenever there was no offspring, the inheritance went to the brothers of the deceased. If, however, daughters only survived, the conservative tribal and family instinct, to which reference has already been made, here came in as a limiting principle. The daughters were allowed to inherit, but the express condition was imposed that they could only marry into the clan of their father's tribe, 'so that the inheritance of the Israelites should not pass round from tribe to tribe, but the Israelites shall cleave each one to the inheritance of the tribe of his fathers, and every daughter that obtains an inheritance among the tribes of Israel shall become the wife of a man belonging to her father's clan and tribe, in order that the Israelites may possess each one the inheritance of his fathers' (Num. xxxvi. 7, 8). This tendency to prevent the alienation of land from the family clan, which in many, if not most, cases would be a local community, may be observed in the law respecting jubilee in Leviticus xxv. 10–28, which ensured that land should not be sold in perpetuity out of the clan, but should revert in the fiftieth year.

In relation to these provisions respecting inheritance by women it is very difficult to determine how far they were operative in pre-exilian times. It should be noticed, however, that Boaz, who is described as belonging to the same clan as Elimelech, husband of Naomi, marries Ruth the Moabitess as joint owner with Naomi of the land belonging to the deceased Elimelech, 'to raise up the name of the dead upon his inheritance,' and it is possible that the law contained in Deuteronomy xxv. 5–10, which required that a *widow* without a son should be married by her husband's brother, may have been enacted not merely to raise up male posterity, but in order to guarantee the continuance of any property she might possess in the clan to which her husband belonged. On the other hand, the absence of any express regulation respecting female inheritance in the Book of Deuteronomy, and the repeated reference to the widow in connection with the orphan and the stranger (Deut. xiv. 29, xvi. 11, xxvi. 12 foll.) as participating in tithes and festival offerings, renders it only too probable that the position of the widow in pre-exilian times was a precarious one. And this may also be gathered from Isaiah x. 2, Jeremiah vii. 6; comp. Zech. vii. 9, 10.

In primitive Israel women possessed as their own personal property not only their clothing but also their jewels. These in fact were the gifts bestowed on the bride by the bridegroom before marriage, as we learn from the case of Rebekah (Gen. xxiv. 22, 53; comp. xxxiv. 12). But there may have been additional gifts bestowed by her own family. From the case of Sarah we learn that it was also possible for her to own a female slave (Gen. xvi. 2, 6, 8, 9). These possessions would vary according to the wealth of the family to which she belonged. The jewels probably constituted the most important part of her property, as is the case at the present day in Southern India. In pre-exilian Israel these items of personal property appear to have formed the utmost sum total of a woman's possessions, as a general rule. In many cases the widow's raiment would be her most important possession. Hence the benevolent legislation of Deuteronomy xxiv. 17 directed that a widow's raiment was not to be taken in pledge.

After the exile the status and rights of women improved among the Jews, and this was probably owing to the influences of Babylonian life upon them. Prof. Sayce has shown[1] that polygamy was not prevalent among the Babylonians, as among other Semitic peoples, and the wife could hold and dispense property apart from the husband. Marriage was also attested by a legal document. These traditions influenced Jewish practice. Comp. Tobit vii. 14.

The unique position of the **firstborn son** in a Hebrew household was expressed by a special name. According to the enactment in Deuteronomy xxi. 17 his special rights in the matter of inheritance consisted of a double portion. But the form in which the enactments in the Deuteronomic code (verses 15–17) are preserved shows that they were intended to be corrective of lax and arbitrary procedure in the apportionment of property. That the claims of the firstborn son were in some way recognised in the primitive tradition of Semitic nations is shown by the fact that Assyrian as well as Hebrew and Aramaic designated the firstborn son by what is essentially the same word. It is evident, however, not only from the language of the passage cited above from Deuteronomy, but from the examples furnished in Scripture narrative, that as the result of polygamy and

---

[1] *Social Life among the Assyrians and Babylonians*, p. 46 foll. A good example of property willed to a daughter may be found in Peiser's *Keilschriftliche Actenstücke*, p. 18 foll. The names of women constantly appear in Babylonian documents; comp. *ibid.*, pp. 26, 44 (dealing with a field which was dowry of a Babylonian lady in the reign of Darius), 48, 53.

the prevailing influence of a favourite wife, or from other causes, the rights which belonged to a firstborn were not infrequently denied to him. Instances may be found in Genesis xxvii., xlviii. 1-20. The example of Ishmael can hardly be cited in this connection, as it is scarcely probable that the rights of a firstborn were ever, except in very extreme cases, granted to the eldest, if he happened to be born of a concubine, unless no male issue from a freeborn wife existed. That this view prevailed in ancient Israel may be inferred from Genesis xxv. 6. This passage, however (as well as Gen. xxi. 10), shows that even sons of concubines *might* share in the inheritance.

7. In dealing with the ancient Hebrew household we have had occasion to refer to the presence of **slaves.** The primitive condition of social life depicted in the Books of Judges and Samuel does not present to us such marked distinctions between the varied classes of the community as are to be observed in nations of a more advanced type of civilization. High and low were equally engaged in pastoral or agricultural employment. They came into very close and hourly contact, and stood upon a more nearly equal footing in respect of culture. The state of society prevailing in Israel prior to the tenth century closely approximated the simple and primitive rural life of Ithaca described in the latter portion of the Odyssey. Just as the Italian Cincinnatus, in the earliest days of the Roman commonwealth, was called to the dictatorship straight from the plough, so the Benjamite Saul was returning with a yoke of oxen from his field when the deputies from Jabesh Gilead arrived (1 Sam. xi. 5). It is certain that the general type of

civilization of the Canaanites (Phœnicians) was much more developed. These were largely town dwellers, and practised many arts and manufactures at a time when the Israelites were engaged almost exclusively in pastoral or agricultural pursuits. But even in early Israel there was one strongly marked contrast, which, though it did not prevent free intercourse, nevertheless entered deeply into the social life of the time. We refer to the two classes of *freemen* (who would be nearly always landowners) and *slaves*. In our advanced modern civilization slavery can be nothing else but a demoralizing curse. This cannot be said of the early social conditions depicted in Judges and Samuel. Life was then less complex, and thus brought master and slave into much closer and more human relationships.

The Hebrew slave was a member of his master's household, for whom the master would care as for his own children. As we have already seen, in the polygamous life of the East, a female slave (like Hagar) could attain to the privileges of a mother of male offspring who might possibly inherit. She might even come, through the death of the freeborn wife, to the attainment of the privileges and dignities of a mistress of the household. It must also be remembered that in the Hebrew household the distinction between Freeborn and Slave was considerably modified by the fact that both alike were regarded by ancient Hebrew custom as the possession of the husband. The relative position assumed by the slave to the rest of the household was therefore by no means so intolerable as we might suppose from modern examples or ancient Roman analogy. The high position attained by Eliezer in the household of Abraham was probably not very exceptional, and his example is to be specially noted, as he is spoken of as a foreigner (a Damascene). It teaches us, moreover, that it was even possible for a slave to inherit his master's property (Gen. xv. 2; comp. Prov. xvii. 2). The Hebrew slave Joseph rose to be prime minister of Egypt. Slaves might even hold property, though to what extent is uncertain, for we find Saul's slave offering one quarter of a shekel, which he had with him (about 8*d*.) in order to pay the seer. It was even possible for a trusted slave to receive a daughter of the house in marriage (1 Chron. ii. 34).

But the lot of a slave would vary with circumstances. Eliezer was born and bred in Abraham's household, and he was entrusted with the delicate commission of conducting the negotiations preliminary to marriage on behalf of his aged master's son, Isaac. Far different would be the position of a recently purchased slave, who had been taken captive in war. Such an one in a Roman household would be set to do the menial tasks, and his place in a Hebrew family would be similar, though not so forlorn. Moreover, the fact that the slave belonged to a different race from his master would aggravate his situation. Slaves of foreign origin were undoubtedly very numerous in the East. Assyrian inscriptions as well as the historical portions of the Old Testament abundantly testify to the barbarous practices that prevailed in Asiatic warfare, when cities were stormed and sacked. We know from numerous inscriptions of monarchs like Ramman-nirâri, Tiglath Pileser, and Sargon, that a large number of the prisoners were carried off as captives. Many of these, of whom females would constitute a considerable proportion —especially those of youth and beauty—would inevitably find their way to foreign markets. The great mercantile Canaanite or Phœnician race, which had their celebrated emporia of commerce at Tyre and Sidon, and possessed a naval supremacy in the Mediterranean from the tenth till the fifth century,[1] shared with the Philistines the unenviable notoriety of being the great slave-dealing race of antiquity. Thus we find the prophet *Amos*, in the middle of the eighth century, bringing this charge against the Philistines, who passed their captive Israelites on to the Edomites. The latter, we may conjecture, may have sold them again to traders, who shipped them from Elath. A similar charge is brought by this prophet against the Phœnicians, against whom a like penalty is denounced, because they forgot the covenant of 'brethren,' which subsisted between Phœnicia and Israel from the days of Solomon downwards[2] (Amos i. 9, 10). Still later we find the pro-

---

[1] As may be learned from 1 Kings v., ix. 26-28; Isaiah xxiii.; Ezekiel xxvii., and Herodotus, Books vi. to viii. *passim*. The following, in Book vii. 96 *ad init.*, is significant: τούτων δὲ ἄριστα πλωούσας παρείχοντο νέας Φοίνικες καὶ Φοινίκων Σιδώνιοι, whereby we learn that the best vessels of Xerxes' expeditionary navy in 480 B.C. were furnished by the Sidonians. Abundant incidental evidence is furnished by the Greek tragedians. Prof. Sayce thinks that the object of the Assyrian wars on the western or Palestinian frontier was to destroy the trade of Phœnicia and divert it to Assyria. This assertion needs proof; and if such was the endeavour, history shows that it failed.

[2] Prof. Wilkins (*Phœnicia and Israel*, p. 119) has drawn attention to this branch of Phœnician commerce: 'The chorus of the Helena of Euripides is composed of maidens who had been brought to the Egyptian market by Phœnician merchants.' The doubts thrown out by Wellhausen (*Skizzen u. Vorarbeiten*,

phet *Joel* inveighing bitterly against both these nations not only for carrying off the silver and gold of Judah, but also for selling the captives of Jerusalem beyond seas to the sons of Javan, *i.e.* to the Greek populations that covered the western shores of Asia Minor.

The average *price* of a slave may be inferred from Exodus xxi. 32 to have been thirty shekels, or about £4, in the early pre-exilian period. But the price would, of course, vary considerably. Joseph's brethren were content with twenty shekels when he was sold to the Ishmaelites (Gen. xxxvii. 28). From the evidence of the Assyrian and Babylonian tablets it appears that prices ranged from about these sums and even lower to considerably higher amounts. 'Thus in the time of Nebuchadnezzar we hear of a woman, Sakinna, and her daughter, a little girl of three years of age, being sold for thirty-five shekels' (about £4 14s.), while a slave woman and 'her son upon her breast' fetched nineteen shekels, or about £2 10s., at the same period. In another case, a husband and his wife fetch fifty-five shekels, or seven pounds (Sayce). Mr. Pinches, of the British Museum, has transcribed for us a contract tablet, in which a slave is sold for $2\frac{2}{3}$ manehs of silver, more than £22.[1] This slave must have been particularly valuable, probably owing

Heft v. p. 69) against Amos i. 9. 10 on account of close similarity to the preceding verses appear to me unjustifiable in an oracle so characterized by repetitions of phrase. The omission of any mention of other Phœnician towns beside Tyre in the course of two verses, when we find this to be the only city mentioned by Ezekiel in the first of his two oracles against Tyre (Ezek. xxvi.), consisting of twenty-one verses, is surely not significant.

[1] *Hebraica*, vol. viii. p. 134 foll. According to Tiele a slave might even cost as much as £95. (*Babylon-Assyrische Geschichte*, p. 507.)

to his possession of some skilled qualifications. The price indicated in the Book of the Covenant (Exod. xxi. 32), cited above, probably indicates the average market value in Western Asia. We find that about the same price was paid centuries later in the Maccabæan period, for we read that Nicanor attempted to defray the Roman tribute of 2,000 talents by the sale of captive Jews at the rate of ninety per talent (2 Macc. viii. 9, 10). Let us note that it was for thirty pieces of silver (shekels) our Lord was sold by the traitor disciple into the hands of His persecutors.

The state of slavery was brought about not only by the reverses of war, but by the dire exigencies of poverty, and other causes. From Leviticus xxv. 25, 39 we learn that voluntary servitude was not infrequent as a means of discharging the debts of poverty; indeed, the claims of the creditor during the regal period became so harsh and exacting, that if the father died his sons might be made into bondslaves in order to pay the debt (2 Kings iv. 1). In postexilian times the evils occasioned by this system brought about a violent reaction, and Nehemiah was able to use his authority in bringing about at least a modification of the practice (Neh. v. 1-13). It is not improbable that we may here see an indirect result of the more humane civilization of Babylonia.[1]

---

[1] Babylonia, as Prof. Sayce (*ibid.*) points out, was a land where agricultural pursuits were carried on, as in Egypt, by industrious, peace-loving freedmen (not by slaves, as in Assyria, where the pursuits preferred by the dominating race were trade and war). Babylonia, moreover, was a land of book-culture. 'The ancient Accadian law ordered that if children had been born to slaves whom their former owner had sold while still keeping a claim upon them, he should, in buying them back, take the children as well, at the rate of 1½ shekels each.' Note

But the influence of the spirit of the Deuteronomic legislation was far more potent. Even the primitive and brief code called the *Book of the Covenant* (Exod. xx. 22–xxiii.) shows that many mitigating circumstances entered to ameliorate the lot of the slave. Among these may be mentioned the *Sabbatic year of release* (Exod. xxi. 2–6), which limited the period of bondservice to six years. In the seventh year the slave became a free man, and had the right to take his wife with him, if married. But here unfortunately his rights became limited. If the wife was his master's slave, both she and her children remained with his master. What happened to the wife and children if the wife were not his master's slave but another's, we are not told, and the silence is ominous.[1] Under these circumstances it is not surprising that the ties of family often prevented the slave from availing himself of the proffered sweets of freedom. Moreover, his position in many cases, especially if he belonged to the same race as his master, was by no means one of hardship. It might indeed be less irksome to him to remain in the master's household, especially if the latter were a wealthy as well as humane

the instances above quoted of mother and child being sold together, also the superior rights accorded to women in the possession of property, as compared with the ancient Palestinian usages. There are numerous instances, moreover, of slaves holding property.

[1] Such is the usage depicted in the *Book of the Covenant*. But the *Deuteronomic legislation* allows the same rights in the Sabbatic year of release to the *woman* as to the man (Deut. xv. 12 foll.) The *Levitical* legislation, with its law of Jubilee, goes a step farther. In the year of jubilee, man, wife *and children* return to their clan and its landed possession (Lev. xxv. 40, 41). It should be observed that these rights were enjoyed only by *Hebrews*.

man, and be maintained in tolerable comfort, than to be obliged in times of scarcity to find his own livelihood. Under these circumstances the slave at the close of the six years would often prefer to remain a slave. The formality observed in such a case was that he and his master should repair to the local sanctuary, where the officials (probably priests) who witnessed the act ratified it in the name of God. The slave testified his desire to forego his right, and abide permanently with his master, who in token of possession bored a hole through the slave's ear.[1] The same thing was done to the female slave. As we turn to the expanded form of this enactment in the Deuteronomic legislation, we again observe the humanitarian touch which characterizes that code. 'And when thou lettest him go free from thee, thou shalt not let him go empty; thou shalt furnish him liberally from thy flock, and out of thy threshingfloor, and out of thy winepress: as the Lord thy God hath blessed thee thou shalt give unto him.' In the Levitical legislation the same spirit manifests itself. The master is exhorted to treat his slave, if a Hebrew, not as a slave, but as a hired servant and sojourner, who is not to be rigorously dealt with. But no such admonition applies to a foreign bondservant.

Another point on which ancient Hebrew legislation protected the slave was personal maltreatment. On this the early compend of laws called the 'Book of

[1] The same custom prevailed among the Arabs, Lydians (Xenoph., *Anab.*, iii. 1. 31) and Carthaginians (Plautus, *Pænulus*, v. 2, 21). The *aures anulatæ* mentioned by Plautus suggest that the hole was bored in the Hebrew slave's ear that it might receive an ear-ring. Similar customs among other nations, with citations, may be found in Dillmann's commentary *ad loc*.

the Covenant,' is very explicit. Injury to eye or tooth of a bondservant wilfully committed by his master received compensation by the immediate gift of freedom (Exod. xxi. 26, 27). If he were murdered, the Levitical legislation prescribed the death penalty, as it would if the victim were free born (Lev. xxiv. 17, 22). Here we notice an advance on the legislation of the Book of the Covenant (Exod. xxi. 20).

Yet with all this the slave was regarded and treated as the master's purchased chattel. And so in fact he was called in the Hebrew language (Gen. xvii. 23; Exod. xii. 44; Lev. xxv. 45). The growth of civilization during the monarchical period tended to aggravate rather than improve the position of the small peasant freeholder. The land became 'full of silver and gold' (Isa. ii. 7). Palestine is geographically the highway of commerce between Egypt and Arabia on the south, and Phœnicia, Syria and Assyria on north and west. The close relations between Israel and Phœnicia, the great mercantile race of the North, stimulated the trade and civilization of the former. But all this tended to destroy the old pastoral and agricultural simplicity of the earlier days. A more highly civilized town life was growing up in Samaria and Jerusalem. Meanwhile the exhausting wars with Syria in the ninth century, and with Tiglath Pileser and Sargon in the eighth, would fall very seriously upon the cultivator of the soil. Personal wealth gave its possessor a fatal power over the poverty-stricken farmer. Usury in Babylonia, and probably in Canaan as well, claimed its twenty per cent., and the result was that the freeholder fell into the clutches of the wealthy noble.

All these evils are reflected in the oracles of Amos, Hosea, and Isaiah (see especially Amos ii.–vi., and Isaiah i.–x. *passim*), where lordly and insolent wealth is portrayed side by side with abject poverty. Amos rebukes the harsh creditor who sells into slavery the innocent debtor for a paltry claim equivalent to a pair of sandals (ii. 6; viii. 6), while Isaiah deplores the aggregation of landed properties into a few grasping hands, and the dispossession of the crushed and poverty-stricken cultivator of the soil (Isa. v. 8). It is true that there were enactments which tended to mitigate the severity of the creditor's power (Exod. xxii. 25 foll.; Deut. xxiii. 19) by limiting its operations to the principal of the debt (Exod.) or to aliens (Deut.); but the very existence of these restrictions indicates the prevalence of the evils they were intended to arrest. There can be little doubt that slavery largely increased during the regal period, and that its conditions became aggravated.

Under the stress of these conditions temptations were not wanting for a slave to escape from the hands of an overbearing and tyrannical master into another tribe or adjoining state, and this would become easier in the days when the Hebrew realm was broken up into two kingdoms, and still later, when the frontiers were curtailed by the encroachments of Assyria. It is to be specially noted that Hebrew law as preserved in the Pentateuch nowhere prescribes it as a duty to deliver up a runaway slave to his owner. It is characteristic of the beneficent Deuteronomic legislation that it sets forth the precise contrary. 'Thou shalt not deliver up a slave to his master, who escapes to thee from his master. With thee shall he abide in thy midst, in the place that he chooses, in any one of thy gates that he likes. Thou shalt not oppress him.' This is in full accord with the sacred rights of hospitality which prevailed among primitive Semitic nations and in primitive Greece. To this we shall refer subsequently. From these facts we may infer that the recovery of a runaway slave in ancient Israel was by no means an easy matter (comp. 1 Kings ii. 39), and this very circumstance would tend to mitigate the slave's lot by making it desirable for the master to render his servant's life tolerable. Another element which entered to bind the slave to his master's household was religion. For it was evidently the custom of the slave to accept the religion and religious rites of his lord. Eliezer of Damascus concludes a contract with his master, in which the name of Jehovah, in accordance with tradition, was solemnly invoked. We also know that he appealed to Jehovah for help in the delicate task which Abraham had set him. This acceptance by a slave of the religion of the household and clan in which he lived was part of the universal system that prevailed in antiquity. Religion was then local, and the cultus of the local clan was adopted by any one who sojourned among its people, since the deity was regarded as potent in the area of which he was regarded as patron and lord.[1] Hence we find that circumcision was also practised on the slave members of the household (Gen. xvii. 23, 27). Thus the slave participated in the clan festivals in fellowship with his master, and shared in the privileges of that common protection which all

---

[1] Illustrations of this conception may be found 1 Samuel xxvi. 18 foll.; Ruth i. 6, 15, 16; 2 Kings xvii. 25 foll.

the members of the clan enjoyed. He also participated in the Sabbath rest (Exod. xx. 10., xxiii. 17; Deut. xvi. 14).

It is time that a few words should be said on the status of a *female* slave. On the whole, her position was more favourable than that of the male bondservant. This was due to the fact that she might become the concubine of the master of the household or of one of his sons. Doubtless there is something to our modern sentiment that is disagreeable in the notion that the master of the household should have absolute control over the person of his female slave, as though she were a chattel. But it must be recollected that in a Canaanite or Hebrew household, the position of a slave woman in this respect was not very different from that of a free woman. We have already had occasion to notice that a maiden, though free, had no power to dispose of herself as she chose.

Language is an important index respecting ancient usage, and differences of name will never arise unless occasioned by diversity of signification, which in this case points to diversity of function and social standing. Hebrew possesses a word (*amah*) almost identical in form with what is really the same word in all the Semitic languages (Assyrian, Arabic and Aramaic). The ancient Israelite girl became *âmah* when sold by her father. This must have taken place among the poorer classes not unfrequently during the regal period, and under the adverse circumstances described on a previous page (36). It often happened that the daughter could not be disposed of as freeborn in ordinary marriage, and could not be supported in the household. She would then be sold as a concubine. But as a concubine she had the right to be treated as a wife; and if she bore male children her position sensibly improved, as has been already explained. But the position of a *shifchah* in a Hebrew household was much lower. This may be gathered from the speech of Abigail (1 Sam. xxv. 41). She calls herself *âmah*, and consents to become a *shifchah*, and do the menial task of washing the feet of David's slaves. It was to the *shifchah* the laborious duty was delegated of grinding at the mill. This is the word used in the original for the slave girl behind the millstones in Exodus xi. 5, where the term is employed to describe the lowest end of the social scale.

There is another strange word used in Hebrew to describe a concubine, viz., *Pillegesh* (Gen. xxii. 24, xxxv. 22; Judges xix. 1; 2 Sam. xv. 16, xx. 3), which is probably to be regarded as a loan word, borrowed from some Indo-germanic language, probably Greek.[1] It therefore signified originally a foreign concubine. But this distinctive meaning does not appear in the Old Testament.

8. **Clothing.** Having described the inmates of a Hebrew household, we shall proceed next to deal with their externalities. Among these, the first to engage our attention will be the *clothing*. Unfortunately this is a subject involved in some uncertainty, as we

---

[1] Compare the Greek πάλλαξ, παλλακίς, Lat. *pellex*. It is difficult to see how the editors of Gesenius' Lexicon (tenth ed.) could have regarded a word so distinctly non-Semitic in type as *borrowed by the Greeks from the Semitic*. Stade is unquestionably right in maintaining that the reverse is the case. The point is important, as it indicates an early contact between the Canaanites and the Greeks, or 'Sons of Javan.'

have comparatively few monumental representations of the dress actually worn by the Hebrews of Palestine in early pre-exilian days. Under these circumstances we have to rely on : (1) the statements of the Old Testament ; (2) the abundant illustrative material of the paintings in Egyptian tombs, and the sculptures of Assyria and Babylonia ; (3) the dress of modern Orientals, especially of the Arabs.

In the earliest times wool and skins would be the materials chiefly employed in the construction of garments. And of this we have an example in the primitive costume of the prophet Elijah. His broad, hairy mantle was probably made from the skins of sheep or goats, and was characteristic of the pastoral life of early Israel,[1] as well as of the ascetic simplicity of the prophetic order which adopted this mode of attire (Zech. xiii. 4 ; Matt. iii. 4). His girdle was likewise of leather. That goats' skins were so used, we may gather from Rebekah's device (Gen. xxvii. 16; comp. Heb. xi. 37). That wool was largely employed in early times for clothing may be inferred from the references to sheep-shearing (Gen. xxxi. 19, xxxviii. 12), and the existence of a religious festival in primitive Israel connected with it (2 Sam. xiii. 23 foll.). A portion of Mesha's tribute consisted of wool (2 Kings iii. 4), and it is mentioned among the offerings of firstfruits, not only by Hosea (ii. 7–11), but also in

---

[1] 'Over the *Kamise* [or unbleached calico shirt] the Syrian shepherd, in wet or cold weather, or during the night, like all other peasants, wears a thick, warm, sleeveless, sack-like outer garment, made of camel's hair, invariable as to material, shape and colour, the latter being dark brown of different shades, with whitish perpendicular stripes. This is the common overcoat of the agricultural labourer, and of all the working classes of the country districts.'—NEIL, *Palestine Explored*, footnote p. 255.

Deuteronomy xviii. 4. That clothing in ancient times largely consisted of woollen garments, is evident from such passages as Job xxxi. 19, 20, and in the later period of the Jewish commonwealth it was regarded as the business of a good housewife in a well-appointed household to be able to spin the wool and manufacture garments (Prov. xxxi. 13). That weaving was practised by the women of the household during the regal period is clearly shown by 2 Kings xxiii. 7, where we learn that the sanctuaries, consisting of tents or curtained apartments, for the licentious worship of Asherah, were 'woven' by the Hebrew women. How far weaving is involved in the reference to the 'small robe' which Hannah 'made' for her son Samuel (1 Sam. ii. 19) is not clear, though the expression probably includes it.

It is certain that at an early period clothing consisting of other material than wool was imported and worn by the Israelites. For the Hebrews were close neighbours of a more highly civilized Canaanite population that occupied the coast-land of Palestine. Immediately to the north were the great centres of commerce, Tyre, Sidon and Damascus. The recent discovery of the cuneiform tablets at Tell el Amarna in Egypt has revealed the significant fact that Babylonian influence and civilization largely prevailed throughout Western Asia, and especially among the populations of Canaan, during the centuries that immediately preceded the invasion of the country by Joshua. Thus in comparatively early times large 'Shinar mantles' or cloaks, such as that discovered by Achan amid the spoil (Josh. vii. 21), would be among the garments imported from Babylonia that were purchased and worn by the more wealthy among the Israelite freemen.

Some of these imported garments were made of 'vegetable wool' or cotton, especially the tunic, called by the Hebrews *sâdin*, a light under-garment worn next to the skin, which is identical with the Babylonian *sindu* (according to Prof. Sayce, made of Indian muslin or cotton). This word and thing were borrowed by the ancient Greeks, and called by them σινδών (*sindôn*). In most cases, however, the *sâdin* was probably woven from the flax (*pishtah*), which largely grew in Egypt, but was likewise a product of Palestinian soil. The stalks of the flax plant were gathered and stored upon the roofs of Canaanite dwellings (Josh. ii. 6). Probably the thirty *sâdin* garments which Samson wagered (Judg. xiv. 12, 13) were made from flax, and were of Philistine rather than Hebrew manufacture. That the Philistines understood the art of weaving in the days of the Judges, is clearly shown by the language of Judges xvi. 13 foll. Both Canaanites and Philistines were at this time considerably in advance of the Hebrews in the arts of civilization. Of this we have a hint in 1 Samuel xiii. 19.

Various names were employed to designate the different materials of flax and cotton. An ordinary form of *flax* was called *bad*, from which the *ephods* of Samuel and David were made (1 Sam. ii. 18; 2 Sam. vi. 14). In later times the Hebrews became acquainted with the fine variety of Egyptian cotton, which they called *shēsh*. It has been supposed, however, that a fine sort of flax is also designated by this term. It was the material of which Joseph's official robes were made (Gen. xli. 42). Later still, in post-exilian times, this fine cotton was called *bûtz*, probably an Aramaic word; and this term again, like others, has been borrowed by the ancient Greeks from the same source from which they gained their alphabet. They called it *byssus* (βύσσος).

Dyeing was not practised in Israel. It was a foreign art. We know from classical writers that the fame of Tyrian purple spread far and wide through all the countries bordering on the Mediterranean reached by Phœnician merchantmen (*Verg., Æneid*, iv. 262; Strabo, xvi. 2, 23). In the days of Ezekiel (sixth century B.C.) it was Syria that supplied both purple and broidered work to the Tyrian market (xxvii. 16; comp. Ps. xlv. 14). In later times some of these arts were learned by Hebrew women of high rank. This, at least, we may probably infer from Proverbs xxxi. 19, 22.

> 'She putteth her hands to the distaff,
> And her palms lay hold on the spindle. . . .
> She prepareth for herself cushions;
> Fine linen and purple is her raiment.'

But in earlier times—such as those to which the Song of Deborah belongs—these expensive luxuries would be purchased by the wealthier Hebrews in return for cattle and agricultural produce. Hence the coloured garments and broidered work that the princesses vainly hoped that Sisera's host would bring them from the routed Hebrews (Judg. v. 30) were undoubtedly the skilled product of foreign looms and handiwork.[1]

---

[1] Stade asserts that purple garments were never worn by the Hebrews in the early period. Judges viii. 26 he puts aside as a gloss. But this sweeping assertion requires proof, though we

The garments of Hebrew men and women were of different shapes and sizes, and must have varied, not merely according to the rank and wealth of the person, but also according to the period in which he lived. In early and primitive Israel we have mainly two articles of clothing: the *upper* or *outer garment* made of wool, called a *simlah*, which corresponded to the *himation* (ἱμάτιον) of the Greeks and to the Roman *toga*. It consisted of a large rectangular piece of woollen cloth, something like a Scotch plaid, which served not only to wrap up the body, but also for the conveyance of sundry articles in its folds. Thus in Exodus xii. 34 we read that the baking troughs or platters were carried by the Israelites in their hurried departure from Egypt upon their shoulders wrapped in the ample folds of this outer garment. The *simlah* was also used to sleep in. Hence the early legislation contained in the Book of the Covenant (Exod. xxii. 26) commands that if this garment be taken in pledge, it shall be restored before sunset, because it is the poor man's only covering for the night. The same fact is apparent from Deuteronomy xxii. 17. (Comp. Job xxii. 6.) On the other hand, the *under garment* worn next to the skin, called *kuttoneth*, was usually of linen (occasionally of wool). This corresponds to, and indeed is in reality, the same word as the Greek *chitôn* (χιτών), which, like the words *byssus* and *sindôn*, was borrowed by the Greeks from the East. This shirt or blouse did not reach beyond the knees, and was either sleeveless or

may accept as true in the main his general statement that the clothing of the Hebrews in early times was made from the products of the country, wool and flax. (*Gesch.*, p. 372.)

provided only with short sleeves.[1] In ordinary occupations in the house or upon the field this would be the sole garment worn, fastened by a girdle.[2] In this condition, according to Biblical language, a man would be called 'naked' or stripped, and it is in this sense we are to understand the command to Isaiah (xx. 2) and the reference to Peter in John xxi. 7.

These were the essentials of ancient Hebrew clothing, but of these there were numerous varieties, according to the rank or occupation of the wearer. Thus of upper garments the term *lebûsh* or *malbûsh* is frequently used in poetry, and seems to have meant an official or state robe. Such a robe was worn by Joab as military commander (2 Sam. xx. 8), by the priests of Baal (2 Kings x. 22), and by royal attendants (1 Kings x. 5).

We have also the broad flowing mantle or cloak, called *addereth*, made of goat's hide or camel's skin covered by the hair, and ordinarily worn by the prophets. Sometimes it was elaborately worked, and made of fine material, like the Babylonian mantle found by Achan, referred to above (Josh. vii. 21). As this last was probably no other than the long robe or cloak specially characteristic of the Babylonians, and constantly depicted on the monuments, Prof. Sayce's description may be suitably quoted: 'It opened in front, was usually sleeveless, and was orna-

---

[1] Probably the figured representations in Rich's *Dictionary of Roman and Greek Antiquities*, p. 697 foll. (art. "Tunica"), are a fairly close approximation to the actual form of the ancient Hebrew under garment.

[2] 'Both Assyrians and Babylonians, while engaged in manual work or military operations, discarded the long and inconvenient outer robe.'—*Sayce*.

mented at the end with fringes. In walking it allowed the inner side of the left leg to be exposed. Not unfrequently the girdle was fastened round it, instead of round the tunic.'

Another form of upper garment was that worn by the *priests*, called the *ephôd*, which was probably a close-fitting coat, about a yard in length, consisting of a front and hinder portion, fastened by buckles, but these details would vary according to the rank of the priest. Thus, according to the minute descriptions of Exodus xxviii., the high priest's ephod was made by a skilled workman, of fine linen, with purple, scarlet, blue and gold thread interwoven. But the ephod worn by the eighty priests at Nob was made of ordinary linen, and was of a simpler and more primitive make (1 Sam. xxii. 18).

Beneath the ephod the priest wore an upper tunic, called a *me'îl*. This is spoken of in close connection with the ephod in Exodus xxviii. 31, xxix. 5, and also in 1 Samuel ii. 19, where our English version renders the Hebrew name *me'îl* by 'coat.' But such a translation, as well as the rendering 'mantle,'[1] is misleading. The *me'îl* was a long upper tunic, worn not only by priests, but also by nobles (Job i. 20) and by kings (1 Sam. xxiv. 4).[2] The Hebrew name expresses the fact that this garment covered an under garment, shirt or chemise, worn next to the skin, called the *sadîn*, to which reference has already been made.

As a head covering, a turban or *tsanîph* was worn, which probably closely resembled that of the modern

---

[1] Employed by Robertson Smith, *Old Testament in the Jewish Church*, p. 270, and Gesenius' Lexicon.
[2] The LXX. render variously by ἱμάτιον, στολή, διπλοῖς, etc.

Oriental, and consisted, as the name clearly indicates, of bands of linen rolled or wrapped round. The *high priest's* headdress consisted of this in a more elaborate form, called *mitznepheth*, and this is sustained by the account of it given in Josephus. Nobles and kings wore it (Isa. lxii. 3; Job xxix. 14), and even ladies of fashion (Isa. iii. 23). A specially handsome form of headdress was called the *pe'ēr*, though its precise character is not at all clear. It was worn on festive occasions, as weddings (Isa. lxi. 10), and by ladies (Isa. iii. 20).

The dress of *women* in its essentials resembled that of men, and consisted of an under garment or tunic of linen, which, however, was longer than that worn by men, and also an outer garment. In the case of ladies of distinction, like Tamar, daughter of David, the *kuttoneth*, when it formed the *me'īl* or upper tunic of linen, consisted of long sleeves reaching to the wrists, and extending as far down as the feet or ankles;[1] and in Genesis xxxvii. we read that the youthful Joseph wore a similar tunic. Beneath this upper tunic a lady in good position also wore the *sadin*, or light linen under garment, worn next to the skin, which probably did not differ much from that worn by men, which has been already described (comp. Isa. iii. 23). Women also had their *simlah*, or outer robe, worn over the tunic, and made, as we may suppose, in most cases of wool. It is evident from the express commandment contained in Deut. xxii. 5 that a woman's *simlah* was distinct in shape from a man's, but in what respect it is impossible to

---

[1] This is certainly the most probable interpretation of the *kuttoneth passim* in 2 Samuel xiii. 18.

determine. The outer garment, however, existed in many different varieties—more especially during the latter portion of the regal period. This may be inferred from the graphic description given by Isaiah of a Jerusalemite lady of fashion (iii. 18-23) walking along the streets of the city with outstretched neck and tripping gait. Among the outer garments we read of a *wrapper*, such as Ruth wore when she went forth in her best attire to meet Boaz (Ruth iii. 15); and the more elaborate *state robe*, such as Zechariah

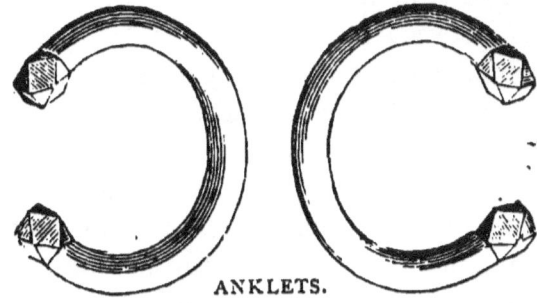

ANKLETS.

(iii. 4) in his vision sees placed upon the high priest Joshua, but is employed by Isaiah as the appropriate word to describe the splendid outer robe of a high-born lady of his time (eighth century B.C.).

The same passage is instructive as revealing the *paraphernalia* which a fashionable woman carried about with her. These we shall proceed to describe. First, we find mention of *anklets*, made of metal, worn round the ankles, which made a tinkling sound as she moved.[1] In connection with these, we must take the

---

[1] 'Anklets (*khulkhal*) of solid gold or silver are worn by some ladies, but are more uncommon than they formerly were. They are, of course, very heavy, and, knocking together as the wearer walks, made a ringing noise; hence it is said in a song, "The ringing of thy anklets has deprived me of my reason."'
—LANE, *Modern Egyptians*.

stepping-chains referred to in verse 20. These probably were connected (as Cheyne supposes) with the anklets. The head was adorned with *bands*, made of gold and silver thread, which passed across the forehead from one ear to the other (Delitzsch). There was also the *pe'ēr*, to which reference has already been made. It may have resembled the *tiara* or head-tire of linen worn by the priest, to which the same name is given in the original. Perhaps the nearest equivalent may be found in the valuable portraiture of Arab attire given to us by Lane. 'The headdress consists of a *tâkeeyeh* and *tarboosh*, with a square kerchief of printed or painted muslin or one of crape, wound tightly round and composing what is called a *rabtah*. Two or more such kerchiefs were commonly used a short time since, and are still sometimes, to form the ladies' turban, but always wound in a high flat shape, very different from the turban of the men.' Next Isaiah mentions the '*crescents*' or 'little moons' (μηνίσκοι, as the LXX. render). These are usually compared with the *hilâlât* or crescents adorning an Arab maiden. The latter are worn as an effective remedy against the evil eye, for, as Delitzsch[1] observes, 'the *hilâl*, or new moon, is

[1] *Commentary on Isaiah*, ad loc. Among modern Arabs 'the *hilâl* is a crescent of diamonds set in gold or silver, and worn like the *reesheh*. In form it resembles the phase of the moon when between two or three nights old, its width being small, and its outward edge not more than half a circle.' But as the *reesheh* was 'worn on the front or side of the headdress,' it is obvious that the *hilâl* was similarly worn. As for the crescents worn on the camels' necks, spoken of in Judges viii. 21, they were unquestionably used as amulets or charms. Lane observes that horses often wear appendages consisting of a few verses of the Korân enclosed in cases of gold, silver, tin, or perhaps leather, and even silk, generally of a triangular form.

the image of growing prosperity.' These crescents were apparently worn hanging as a necklace. (Comp. Judg. viii. 21, where the crescents are described as carried on the necks of the camels of the two Midianite kings, Zebah and Zalmunnah.) It is quite possible, however, that the ancient Hebrew crescent, like the modern Arab *hilâl*, was worn upon the headdress or *pe'ēr*. We come next to the '*ear-drops*,' as the ear-rings are most aptly described, which adorned the males among the Midianites (Judg. viii. 26). Here again Lane's work furnishes us with useful modern analogues (see annexed wood-cut). 'It consists of a

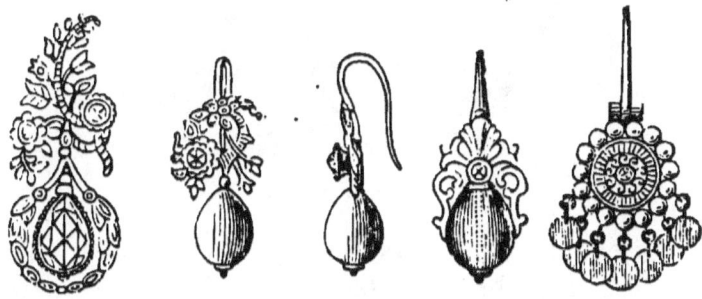

EAR-DROPS.

drop suspended within a wreath hanging from a sprig.' Sometimes it consists of diamonds, sometimes emeralds or rubies, set in silver or gold. In ancient times glass may also have been used, for we know that it was manufactured in Egypt in very early times (Wilkinson, iii. 88 ; comp. Pliny, *Hist. Nat.*, xxxvi. 64 ; xxxviii. 26, 33, 75); and glass bowls have been discovered in Nineveh, as well as glass ornaments in Babylon (Layard, *Nineveh and Babylon*, abridged ed., pp. 65, 290).

Our attention is next taken up by the *nose-rings*, which were very commonly worn by Hebrew women.

As the same word is used in Hebrew for an ear-ring (not 'ear-drop'), we may assume that it was shaped like an ordinary ear-ring. One of these nose-rings was presented by Eliezer to Rebekah (Gen. xxiv. 47). A modern Egyptian nose-ring is depicted in the appended illustration.

NOSE-RINGS.

Orientals, ancient as well as modern, also cherish *amulets*, and these, we learn from Isaiah, were worn by the Hebrew lady (called *lechashim*), and regarded by her as a protection against malign influences. Cheyne, in his comment on the passage (Isa. iii. 20), thinks that by the amulets ear-rings are here meant, and quotes the very significant illustrative passage, Gen. xxxv. 4, where Jacob is described as burying them under the terebinth tree. We know from the Old Testament record how accessible the Hebrews from early times were to superstitious influences, and we have already seen that the 'crescents' were probably used as charms, like their modern analogues. Just as the crescent would be connected with the cultus of the moon goddess Ashtoreth (goddess of love), the amulets would be associated with the worship of other deities, and might contain represen-

FAMILY AND HOUSEHOLD OCCUPATIONS 53

tations of them.[1] The '*scent-cases*' we may fittingly suppose to have been suspended from the 'girdle,' mentioned in verse 20, and probably contained some preparation of the balsam-perfume, since this perfume is specially mentioned in verse 24; but there were many other varieties, as we learn from Psa. xlv., in which we are told that the royal bride's garments were fragrant with myrrh, aloes and cassia (Song of Sol. iv. 14 gives a list of them). The *loose flowing veils*

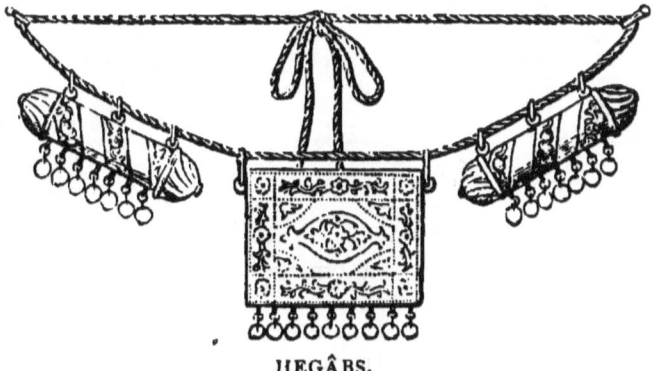

HEGÂBS.

(*re‘alôth*) were evidently made of fine and more elaborate material than the ordinary *tsa‘iph*.

The *sherah* was probably a *bracelet* for the arm (rather than arm chain), and thus meant the same thing, as the same, or nearly the same, word in the modern Arabic, *siwâr*, a bracelet made of precious stones set in gold, or of gold alone. Lastly, the small *hand mirrors*, made of polished metal, which may have

---

[1] Modern Arabic usage, described by Lane in his valuable eleventh chapter on '*hegâbs*,' or charms, suggests the possibility that the ancient Hebrew amulet may have consisted of *words* inscribed upon the stone, as, for example, onyx, or metal of the amulet. According to ancient Semitic ideas, great potency was ascribed to the *name* of a deity, whether uttered or written. (See SAYCE, *Hibbert Lectures*, p. 302 foll.)

resembled the somewhat larger *specula* used by a Roman lady in her toilet, conclude the long list of a Jewish lady's luxuries furnished by the Hebrew prophet of the latter part of the eighth century.

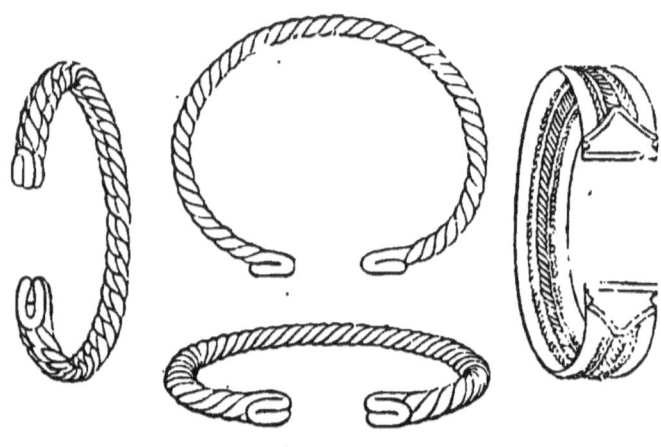

BRACELETS.

There are also two supplementary points to be mentioned in connection with a woman's toilet. The first has reference to the *artistically curled* or *plaited hair*,[1] of which the prophet makes special mention in the same passage (verse 24); and the second is the custom of *painting the eyes*, to which fashionable women, as Jezebel, resorted (2 Kings ix. 30), and which prevailed also in Jerusalem in the days of Jeremiah (iv. 30) and Ezekiel (xxiii. 40). Not only the eyebrows, but also both the eyelids were painted with *stibium* or antimony. In modern Egypt *kohl* is used for this pur-

[1] 'The hair, excepting over the forehead and temples, is divided into numerous braids or plaits; . . . then hung down the back. . . . Over the forehead the hair is cut rather short; but two full locks hang down on each side of the face; these are often curled in ringlets, and sometimes plaited.' —LANE, *Modern Egyptians*.

pose, made of the smoke-black of burned almond-shells, or of an aromatic resin called *libán*. Probably the custom has been simply handed down in Egypt intact through four or five millenniums, for ancient paintings and sculptures exhibit it, and even kohl vessels with the probes and the remains of the black powder have been discovered in ancient tombs.

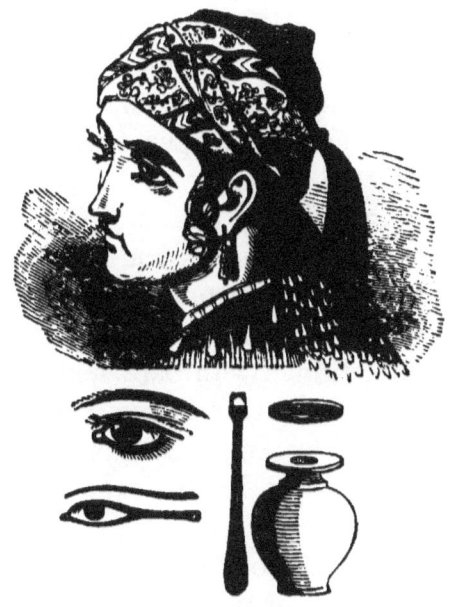

KOHL VESSEL AND PROBE.

The feet were usually shod with *sandals*, which in the main consisted, in ancient times as well as now, of soles of leather or wood tied under the feet by means of thongs (Gen. xiv. 23; Isa. v. 27). This simple arrangement is obviously best adapted to a hot climate, the sandals being easily removed, as this was necessary, according to ancient usage, on entering the presence of a superior or into a sanctuary

(Exod. iii. 5; Josh. v. 15). Cheap sandals were worn even by the very poorest, and their price was so small that Amos uses it as a rhetorical expression for a very low sum (Amos ii. 6; viii. 6). The sandals worn by women of high station were made of finer material; according to Ezekiel xvi. 10 they were of *tachash*-hide, probably *sheep-skin*.[1]

Soldiers also wore sandals, as we learn from Isaiah's graphic description in chapter v. 27, as well as from the Assyrian monuments. The soles were firmly and strongly made, and the back was protected with leather, but the toes and upper portion of the foot were bare, covered only by the thongs that were bound firmly and tightly across. But Prof. Sayce tells us that the Northern conquests of Tiglath Pileser III. and Sargon introduced the laced boot of the inhabitants of the Northern regions. The cavalry, who had hitherto ridden with bare legs, now adopted high boots, laced in front, and worn over tightly-fitting breeches of plaited leather. Certain of the foot soldiers were also clothed in the same way. As this change was introduced in the time of Isaiah, it is probably this kind of boot to which he refers under the word *seôn* in chapter ix. 5, where he speaks of the military costume that is to become the food of devouring flames on the advent of the glorious Messianic King.

---

[1] The same word is found in Assyrian, and Prof. Fried. Delitzsch has shown that the rendering of the corresponding phrase in the inscriptions of Tiglath Pileser I., Asshur-nazir-abal and Shalmaneser II., by '*sheep-skin*' is most probable (*Prolegomena*, p. 77 foll.). Rashi and Luther rendered *badger's skin*, and also our Authorized Version. The translation '*seal skin*' of our Revised Version is improbable.

In ancient as in modern times the fingers were adorned with *rings*. Indeed, these had an official significance. Thus Pharaoh presented Joseph with a ring when he was invested with authority (Gen. xli. 42). The reason for this was that the ring was used as a seal. It was also frequently inscribed with the name of the owner,[1] and was worn on the right hand, as Jeremiah xxii. 24 clearly shows. Seal rings were likewise worn by women, and the list of ornaments in Isaiah iii. 18-23 contains them. Respecting their use in attesting documents we shall speak later on (see below, § 23).

9. **Dwellings.** From the clothing and ornaments of the ancient Hebrews we shall now pass to describe their dwellings. As in the case of clothing, we shall observe that the growth of civilization as well as surrounding influences, especially Canaanite or Phœnician, tended to introduce greater elaboration and complexity of detail. The earliest dwellings of which the Old Testament gives us any hint are the *caves* or *holes* in the rocks, indicated by the name of the primitive race of Horites (Deut. ii. 12, 22 ; Gen. xiv. 6), which signifies in the original cave dwellers or troglodytes. Under the stress of poverty or famine, men in comparatively civilized life tended to lapse into such modes of existence (Job xxx. 3-6). We know that

---

[1] The inscription on a seal ring obtained by M. Oppert at Haleb is cited in Schröder's *Phœnician Grammar*, where several examples of inscriptions on seals and gems are also given. One of these may be quoted. It runs : ' (belonging) to Achothmelech, wife of Jesha ' (p. 273). In a letter to the *Academy* dated Sept. 29, 1889, Prof. Sayce mentions a very interesting seal discovered in Egypt, and apparently belonging to the seventh century, containing the legend, 'to the prosperity of Jeremiah.'

about 400 B.C. Xenophon found entire villages of underground inhabitants in Armenia, whose dwellings were reached by a ladder, and contained sheep, oxen, and fowls as well as corn (*Anabasis*, iv. 5. 25). They even exist at the present day. But among the primitive and nomadic Hebrews the dwellings consisted either of *booths* formed from the branches and leaves of trees, of which the Feast of Booths or Tabernacles formed a religious commemoration, or of *tents*, the prevailing form of habitation in the early patriarchal period and during Israel's sojournings in the wilderness.

Dwelling in booths largely prevailed in the time of David. From the language of Uriah the Hittite (2 Sam. xi. 11, R.V.), this was evidently the case in times of war. David himself had a house with the usual flat roof. The old tent life of Israel was commemorated in the famous cry of revolt among the different scattered clans, 'To your tents, O Israel' (2 Sam. xx. 1 ; 1 Kings xii. 16) ; and the same form of dwelling has been preserved among the nomadic Arabs from the earliest days of ancient Israel to the present time.[1] From Arab life our descriptions of the Hebrew tent are derived, as well as from the notices contained in Scripture. The tents were originally made from skins, subsequently from wool or goats' hair, or occasionally camels' hair. The tent-cloth rested upon one or several poles, according to the size of the tent, and

---

[1] In Arabic the word which in Hebrew means 'tent,' is used to express the ideas of 'family' or 'people.' Hebrew, on the other hand, marks a higher advance in civilization by expressing the same ideas by the word 'house' (*bêth*) as 'House of David,' 'House of Israel.' The Egyptians were called 'House of Slavery' (or bondage).

it was firmly fixed to the ground by means of tent-pegs or tent-pins. The latter were driven into the earth by means of a mallet. Both were employed with deadly effect upon Sisera by Jael (Judg. iv. 21, v. 26). The form of the tent varied according to the size—some, and the smaller ones, being round, the larger being oblong. A larger tent would be divided by hangings or carpets into three spaces, the front space being reserved for the commoner people along with the cattle, the second for the male part of the family, while the third or hindermost space was reserved for the women. But in the case of the more important personages there would be a separate tent for each of the wives. Thus Jacob's tent stood apart from Leah's and from Rachel's, while a single tent sufficed for his two concubines (Gen. xxxi. 33). Similarly Sarah had a separate tent of her own (Gen. xxiv. 67).

The tents of the wandering nomad tribes were arranged in circular encampments or movable hamlets, in the midst of which the cattle would be secured,[1] called in Arabic *duwâr*, and in Hebrew *chatsēr*. The latter word is frequently employed in Hebrew proper names of places; for, as the Semites in Palestine passed from a nomadic to a settled life, these encampments became fixed abodes. Even in the southern parts of Judah and east of the Jordan, which was better adapted for flocks than for agricul-

---

[1] See Palmer's *Desert of the Exodus*, vol. ii. p. 321 foll. The word *chatser* is employed in Gen. xxv. 16 to designate the movable settlements of Ishmaelite tribes. As illustrations of its use to designate permanent settlements, see the proper names of places in Judah or South Judah, Num. xxxiv. 4; Josh. xv. 3, 27.

ture, these tent settlements soon gave place to more permanent abodes. Around some tower or *migdal*, built to protect the land and its dwellers against hostile incursions, spaces surrounded by a wall were employed by the owners of flocks and herds, to guard their property against depredation.

As agriculture developed among the Hebrews, these settled habitations became more numerous, while contact with the Canaanite town dwellers, and the conquest of their cities, introduced the Israelites to a superior and more elaborate form of dwelling. The home of the Israelite peasant farmer would still remain the same primitive structure that we now see inhabited by the fellahîn of Palestine, made either of mud or sunburnt bricks, while the wood employed would be the sycamore, the commonest and cheapest timber in Canaan from the days of Solomon onwards (1 Kings x. 27; Isa. ix. 10). Crossbeams plastered with clay formed the flat roof, on which during the night in sultry weather the inmates slept. These simple dwellings would have no storey; *i.e.*, consisted only of a ground-floor, and sometimes contained but one apartment, and even this would serve as a shelter for the cattle during the night, the inmates sleeping upon a raised platform. But in many cases an enclosure for cattle would be attached. The windows 'were small apertures high up in the wall, for the admission of light and air, sometimes furnished with a grating of wood.'[1] Doubtless in

---

[1] So Lane informs us respecting the dwellings of the peasants in Lower Egypt. He also says: 'The inhabitants of the house, who seldom have any night-covering during the winter, sleep upon the top of the oven, having previously lighted a fire within it; or the husband and wife only enjoy this luxury, and the

the period of the Judges and the beginning of the Hebrew monarchy even the wealthier members of Hebrew society lived in simple dwelling houses. From 2 Samuel xiii. 6 foll. it would appear that even in a prince's dwelling the sleeping apartment was but slightly separated from the kitchen, and the latter was the chief room and place of common resort.

The wars of David, and the consolidation of Israel's power in his reign and that of Solomon, gave a considerable impetus to the prosperity and civilization of the realm. One powerful influence that contributed in this direction was the close bond of intercourse and alliance with Phœnicia, which Solomon and subsequent monarchs did their best to foster. We cannot, unfortunately, describe in detail the palace of Solomon, since the account of the 'house of the forest of Lebanon,' or Solomon's palace of cedar wood, contained in 1 Kings vii. 2–12, is very brief and obscure. According to this passage, on which is based the reconstruction attempted by Stade in his *History of Israel*,[1] it consisted of an upper storey as well as a ground floor. We clearly gather from the Biblical text that there was a portico with columns in front, which led to another porch in the rear, containing the throne where the king gave judgment. Both ceiling and floor were of cedar, and ample provision was made for light by means of windows. Attached to this building was a palace

---

children sleep upon the floor.' It may be laid down as a general principle that the lowest forms of civilized life change least from one century or millennium to another.

[1] p. 319 foll.

for Pharaoh's daughter. Solomon's residence, about which our information is so scanty and obscure, was evidently throughout the work of Phœnician craftsmen and artists, and was a great advance upon the habitations Saul and David had lived in. It must have produced a great impression on the Hebrew nation, and stimulated among the upper classes of society a desire for a more exalted style of living. Then in 2 Kings iv. 10 we read that the wealthy household of Shunem made for Elisha an upper room for his convenience and comfort, which probably somewhat resembled the similar chamber built by Eglon, King of Moab, which was provided with folding doors, and used by him as an audience chamber [1] (Judg. iii. 20 foll.).

When we come to the ninth and following centuries, we at once begin to realize from the language of the annalists and prophets that a great change had passed over Israel since the time of Solomon. The causes for this, and the great increase of wealth, have

---

[1] LXX. ὑπερῷον θερινόν, 'upper room used in summer.' The Hebrew signifies 'upper room for cooling.' It is much to be deplored that so many passages in the Old Testament which deal with architectural details are very doubtful both as to text and interpretation. Thus in Judges iii. 23, 'and Ehud went out [from the chamber] into the *misdrôn*, and he closed the folding doors of the upper room.' The Revised Version follows the Authorized in rendering 'porch.' This translation or 'colonnade,' entered through the folding doors, seems fairly probable. All we know for certain is that *misdrôn* means that which contains a *row* of something, whether pillars or steps. If the latter, we ought to think of a staircase. And such a view is supported by the fact that 'a flight of steps open to the air,' as Prof. Sayce tells us, led to the upper storeys of a high-class Babylonian house. Moreover, it would have facilitated Ehud's escape. The conclusion of the preceding verse (22) contains a problematical word, which is obviously a corruption of this same expression *misdrôn*.

been indicated on a previous page (p. 36). Thus, from the account of Jezebel's death in 2 Kings ix. 30 foll., it is evident that the latticed windows with which the royal residence was provided, and from which Jezebel was looking upon the procession below, belonged to the upper storey of the building, and were at a considerable height above the ground, so that the fall of the ill-fated queen wrought instant death. This event occurred in the middle of the ninth century, when Phœnician influence was all-prevalent in the Northern kingdom, and probably in the Southern kingdom as well. From the oracles of Amos and Isaiah we gather that in the middle and towards the close of the eighth century the large landed proprietors of Israel lived in stately houses that were elaborately furnished. From Amos iii. 15 we learn that it was a common custom for a wealthy man to possess not only a winter residence, but also a summer one. The latter would be specially constructed with open courts, upper storeys and latticed windows. Sittingrooms and bedrooms were arranged around an open court, as in Babylonia and Assyria, resembling the Greek *peristyle* or *aula*. Indeed, the general plan of the Greek as well as Roman house was borrowed, like much else, from Western Asia. From Prof. Sayce's instructive work on the *Social Life of Babylonia* we learn that the palaces of Nineveh were adorned with ornamented dados and cornices. The 'ivory mansions' referred to by Amos in the above passage were probably decorated in similar fashion, only we should substitute woodwork for the sculptured stone of Assyria. The woodwork consisted of cedar wood with inlaid ivory. This was probably one of the innumerable details learned from Phœnicia (comp. Ps. xlv. 8). We know from a significant passage in Isaiah (ix. 9, 10) that it was a growing fashion of his time among the wealthier inhabitants of Ephraim to abandon the use of the common sycamore-wood (1 Kings x. 27), and to substitute the more costly cedar. The sundried or the baked bricks previously employed were displaced by the more durable hewn stone. All these forms of architectural improvement were borrowed from Phœnicia, which possessed then, and afterwards the most skilful craftsmen in the world.[1] From the inscriptions of Sargon we learn that it was from Phœnicia and the land of the Hittites he borrowed the form of a certain kind of portico as well as its name,[2] and it was from the same region the cedar wood was transported wherewith Assyrian kings, like those of Israel, loved to garnish their mansions.

In the following, or seventh century, in spite of the devastations wrought by Assyrian invasions, there seems to have been no diminution in the craving for luxury and adornment. Of this Jeremiah gives us a graphic example in his denunciation of Jehoiakim for yielding to this craving. Spacious upper rooms were then the prevailing fashion,

---

[1] Herodotus pays express tribute to the superior ietelligence and capacity of Phœnician workmen in his account of the construction of the canal that was cut across Mount Athos. They 'showed their skill in this, as in other operations' (vii. 23).

[2] Cylinder inscrip., line 64, and Khorsab., 161, 162. The name Hittite was employed loosely as a geographical term, as Schrader has clearly shown. The name (*bît chilâni*) is probably Phœnician. On this subject see the interesting monograph by Meissner and Rost; also their *Bauinschriften Sanheribs* (p. 4).

adorned with a profusion of cedar wood and painted with red ochre. A further detail we learn from the same prophet and other oracles belonging to the closing decades of the seventh century (Jer. xix. 13, xxxii. 29; Zeph. i. 5; comp. 2 Kings xxiii. 12). It was the habit of the wealthier inhabitants of Jerusalem to erect upon the roofs of their houses small shrines to Baal, Ashtoreth and other star deities. Also in the seventh century a parapet or battlement was erected for greater security around the roof (Deut. xxii. 8).

10. To the houses of the rich **pleasure gardens** were attached. We know that Sennacherib laid out a beautiful park close to the 'palace without equal,' of which he gives us an elaborate description. This he planted with cypresses, palms, and all sorts of fragrant plants. A canal is constructed, and also a pond for watering the garden.[1] We may compare with this the description of the pleasure grounds, with fruit trees and pools of water for irrigation, contained in Eccles. ii. 4-6. But it is generally agreed that the Book of Ecclesiastes is late, and probably belongs to the Greek period. We know that the Greeks borrowed their *paradeisos* or park from the Persians, who again borrowed the art of planting gardens from the Babylonians.[2] It is doubtful whether

---

[1] See the text, with transcription and translation, published by Mr. Evetts in *Zeitschrift für Assyriologie*, vol. iii. p. 311 foll. The description of the *paradeisos* begins in lines 85 foll. (pp. 317 foll., 322, 326). See also Meissner and Rost's *Bauinschriften Sanheribs*, pp. 5 and 14 foll.

[2] The 'Song of Songs' also contains numerous passages, notably iv. 12-15, descriptive of the pleasure grounds of the ancient Hebrews, with their orchards of pomegranates and other fruits, as well as their fragrant spice plants. Many modern

E

the ancient Hebrews, before the period of the exile, possessed gardens at all comparable with these, either in extent or elaboration of detail. But it is evident from several passages that the wealthier Hebrews possessed pleasure grounds surrounding their country houses. Thus we read of the burial of Manasseh, as well as of his son Amon, in the garden of Uzzah (2 Kings xxi. 18, 26); and there is a special mention of the king's garden in 2 Kings xxv. 4; while Isaiah i. 29, xvii. 10, gives us a significant and graphic touch, which shows that the 'plants of pleasure' with which these gardens were adorned were probably connected with the sensuous worship of Tammuz or Hadad, the equivalent of the Greek Adonis (comp. Isa. lxv. 3). We read also that Ahab robbed Naboth of his vineyard that he might convert it into a 'garden of herbs.' But the original suggests that the herbs here mean either grass or vegetables of some kind, intended for use rather than enjoyment (2 Kings xix. 26; Deut. xi. 10). It is doubtful whether a pleasure ground can be intended by this phrase.[1] On the other hand, the phraseology in the description of the Garden of Eden (Gen. ii. 8, 9) shows that the writer was familiar with pleasure grounds; and nearly all critics[2] hold that

critics (like Cornill) regard this dramatic idyll as belonging to a late post-exilian period, but the evidence is by no means as decisive as it is in the case of Ecclesiastes. Contact with the civilization of Babylon probably taught the Jews the art of horticulture to a higher degree than they had known it in the pre-exilian period.

[1] Thenius' interpretation of this expression is therefore to be rejected.

[2] The chief exceptions are Prof. Friederich Delitzsch, Paul Haupt, and recently Mr. Fripp, who hold that Babylonian influence is clearly visible in the narratives of the Jehovist writer or writers of Genesis ii. 4–iv., and accordingly infer that this and

the second and following chapters of Genesis (ii. 4–iv.) are of ancient pre-exilian origin. From these scattered indications we can clearly gather that the wealthy land-proprietors of Judah had well-planted gardens, provided chiefly with fruit trees, attached to or surrounding their lordly mansions.

11. Let us now enter the dwellings of the ancient Hebrews, and take note of the **household furniture**. Here the lowest scale of social life and civilization in the Arabian life of the present day will represent the general aspect of the simplest and most primitive Hebrew household. Thus the tent of an ancient Israelite was provided only with an *opening* (as the Hebrew phrase clearly shows), and near the entrance to it the owner would sit at noon, or, as the original calls it, 'the heat of the day.' Lane's description of the household furniture of an Egyptian peasant would accurately describe nearly all that would meet the eye of any visitor to the tents of Israel three thousand years ago: 'The furniture consists of a mat or two to sleep on, a few earthen vessels, and a handmill to grind the corn.' But as we pass from tents to houses built of brick or of stone, our eye would first light upon the door, which swung upon hinges (Prov. xxvi. 14). The hinge probably con-

---

other sections were composed during the exile. The fact of Babylonian influence is admitted by Dr. Schrader, but the inference is denied, as Palestinian traits are also conspicuous. The question is discussed in his *Cuneiform Inscriptions and the Old Testament*, vol. i., Introd., p. xviii. foll., and also p. 41 foll. Much additional light has recently been thrown on this subject by the discovery of the Tell el Amarna inscriptions, which conclusively prove the wide prevalence of Babylonian influence in Western Asia, and especially in Palestine and Lower Egypt, in times anterior to those of Moses and Joshua.

sisted simply of a pivot fitting into a socket, just as in ancient Greek houses. In many cases the doors were double.

Locks and keys, in anything like our modern sense of the term, were unknown. When we read in Judges iii. 23 foll. that Eglon's chamber was bolted and subsequently opened by a key, it would be hardly safe to go to modern Oriental usage for illustration. Lane's description of the lock and corresponding key in a modern Egyptian house appears to us too elaborate, and we should be disposed, therefore, to consider the simpler contrivance, called by the Romans *clavis Laconica*, and described by Rich in his *Antiquities*, from an Egyptian original preserved in the British Museum, as more approximately representing the key that Eglon's servant employed; but in the case we are considering the key was probably not used for raising a latch, as Rich describes it, but by means of the teeth was slipped into corresponding holes or depressions of a long, sliding bolt. Like its Roman equivalent, however, it would be employed from the outside alone, being inserted through a narrow aperture in the door.

As in modern Oriental dwellings, the furniture of a Hebrew house was simple and scanty. From 2 Kings iv. 10 we learn that the upper chamber provided for the convenience of Elisha by the mistress of the wealthy household of Shunem, consisted of a *mittah*, which was probably nothing else but a simple mattress,[1] which would serve the purpose both of bed

---

[1] The *mittah* probably meant originally this, and this only. But in comparatively early times (eighth century) it came also to signify a divan (see Amos vi. 4).

and couch, and could be rolled up and taken away; also a *table*, which stood upon legs, as we may infer from another passage (Judg. i. 7), where Adonibezek speaks of the seventy kings who were deprived of their thumbs, and gathered the morsels that fell beneath his table. We also read of a seat or *chair*, and lastly of a *lamp, lampstand,* or holder. In the case of a small room, like that occupied by Elisha, the lamp would be a very simple one, and would be represented by the clay lamp recently discovered among the ancient Canaanite remains of Tell el Ḥesî (Lachish) by Mr. Flinders Petrie. The clay lamps in poorer Oriental houses are almost identical. Or, if somewhat more elaborate, it would resemble the Roman *lucerna*, which was generally ' made of terra cotta or bronze, with a handle at one end, a nozzle for the wick at the other, and an orifice in the centre for pouring in the oil. . . . When used, it was placed on some other piece of furniture' (Rich). The presence of the lamp, even in the most humble dwelling, was so characteristic and significant, that we find frequent references to it in Old Testament literature. This lamp was never suffered to go out. The Arab dwellers in Palestine at the present day, and also the Bedouin, retain this custom. Probably it arose from a very simple fact. Until comparatively recent times fire and light could only be generated by the laborious process of friction. Consequently, to save the household considerable delay and trouble, either the hearth fire was always kept burning, as among the more northerly races of Greece and Rome, or the lamp was maintained continually alight. Among the ancient Greeks and Romans a ritual significance came to be attached to the former custom. Among the Hebrews the presence of the light in the household, and the sound of the grinding millstones, were both taken to express the fact of the continuance of the family life. The former was especially used to symbolize family prosperity or the reverse, as in the phrase 'The candle of the wicked is put out.' Examples may be found by the reader in Jeremiah xxv. 10; Proverbs xiii. 9, xx. 20, xxxi. 18; Psalm xviii. 28.

In the humbler households, the appliances for producing and preserving food were of a very simple

HANDMILL.

character. Foremost and most universal among them was the *handmill*, by which the meal daily required for household consumption was prepared. We append here a representation, which gives us the form of a modern Arabian *durra* mill. In this the lower stone is adapted for the reception of the grains, which are ground by a smaller stone above it. It is most probable, however, that the primitive Israelites were acquainted with the form of handmill familiar to the ancient Greeks and Romans, and still employed by the inhabitants of Palestine. This consisted of two round stones. Hence the Hebrew name for it (*rechaim*) is a dual, like the corresponding Arabic form. The 'nether' or lower millstone, which received the corn, was convex, and was provided with a projection around which the upper stone, which was concave, revolved, and thus ground and crushed the grains of corn. The upper stone, since it revolved or 'rode' upon the other, was called a *recheb* (Deut. xxiv. 6; 2 Sam. xi. 21).[1] Probably the mortar, with its pestle, was likewise employed, and was the more ancient form of handmill. In any case, the grinding of the daily quota of meal must have been a monotonous and weary task. In describing this part of the domestic life of a Hebrew household, we shall borrow from Layard's graphic description of his encampment among wandering Arabs on the Khabûr.[2] 'The wandering Arabs have no other means of grinding their corn than by handmills, which they carry with them wherever they go. They are always worked by the women, for it is considered unworthy of a man to engage in any domestic occupation. . . . The grain is passed through the hole of the pivot, and the flour is collected in a cloth spread under the mill. It is then mixed with water, kneaded in a wooden bowl, and pressed by the hand into round balls ready for baking. During these processes the women are usually seated on the bare ground. Hence in Isaiah (xlvii. 1, 2) the daughter of Babylon is told to sit in the dust and on the ground, and "to take the millstones to grind meal."' As we have already indi-

---

[1] Stade's *Geschichte Israel's*, p. 367, from which the above details are derived.
[2] *Nineveh and Babylon*, abridged edition, p. 127 foll.

cated in a previous page, in wealthier households this laborious duty was delegated to female slaves, and this fact imparts additional significance to the above passage. The wooden bowl or dish in which the dough was kneaded was called by the Hebrews *mishereth*. It must have been of shallow depth, and of no great size, for we read in Exodus xii. 34, that these kneading bowls (or 'troughs') were carried on the shoulder by the Israelites when they departed from Egypt.

After the kneading came the baking. And here, again, in order to realize the domestic life of Israel in the primitive age, when the nation was almost entirely nomadic and pastoral, we shall have recourse to Mr. Layard's vivid description: 'The tribes who are always moving from place to place bake their bread on a slightly convex iron plate, moderately heated over a low fire of brushwood or camel's dung. The lumps of dough are rolled on a wooden platter into thin cakes a foot or more in breadth, and laid upon the iron. They are baked in a very short time. . . . The Arab tribes that remain for many days in one place make rude ovens by digging a hole in the ground about three feet deep, shaping it like a reversed funnel and plastering it with mud. They heat it by burning brushwood within, and then stick the lumps of dough, pressed into small cakes about half-an-inch thick, to the sides with the hand. The bread is ready in two or three minutes.'

It should be observed that all Arab bread is unleavened. And it is evident that such must have been the prevailing usage in early Israel; otherwise the meal cakes which Abraham ordered Sarah to make with so much despatch for his angel visitors (Gen. xviii. 6) could not have been prepared, and the same remark applies to the cakes made by the witch of Endor for Saul (1 Sam. xxviii. 24). The use of *leaven* in bread came to be adopted at a later stage in the growth of civilization.

The *oven* of the Hebrews—called by them and modern Arabs alike *tannûr*—was a jar about three

MODERN OVEN.

feet high, broad at the bottom and narrow at the top, where the opening was. At the base it was provided with a hole, through which the fire was stirred. Sometimes a jar-shaped erection of this kind was fixed on to the floor of the house. The fuel which was employed for heating it consisted of dry twigs or grass (Matt. vi. 30), or even dung (Jer. vii. 17 foll.; Ezek. iv. 12 foll.), and the flat cakes of dough were plastered, after the oven had been well heated, upon the glowing hot flint stones placed inside the oven. Only a few minutes were necessary for the baking process to be accomplished. Thus it was easy for the baking process to last too long, and for the cakes to become burnt (Hos. vii. 4, 7). Usually such an oven is placed in a separate outhouse or cabin, which a single house might employ for its own use, or would share with several families (Nowack).

We have hitherto described the furniture of the simpler Hebrew dwelling houses. Wealth and growing civilization would multiply the details and add to their elaboration. Thus after the reformation in the reign of Josiah, when the art of writing prevailed very widely, the doorposts of the houses, as well as the public gateways, were inscribed with precepts of the law (Deut. vi. 9, xi. 20). Also within the sleeping chambers of the larger and more stately dwelling houses the *mittah* or mattress would give place to the *'eres*, bedstead or couch; while in the banqueting-room the nobles reclined on *divans* of costly wood inlaid with ivory (Amos vi. 4), in place of the simpler rug or carpet on which their forefathers sat or rested. As houses became built into upper storeys as well as ground floors, it became customary in winter time to provide a 'brazier' (Jer. xxxvi. 22 foll.). This consisted of a vessel placed in the middle of the room in a small depression, so that when the fire had burnt itself out the vessel might be covered up by a frame over which is spread a carpet, so as to retain the heat as far as possible.

12. Among domestic **utensils** the first place must be assigned to the earthenware *kad* (Gen. xxiv,

14; 1 Kings xvii. 12), or *pitcher*. The women and girls, with the *kad* on the shoulder, making their way to or from the well, is a sight to be witnessed through all the millenniums of Eastern life from the days of Rebekah until now, and from Damascus to Cape Comorin. In size these pitchers were from eighteen inches to two feet in height, and were skilfully carried on the head. There were likewise *bottles* made from *goat skin* employed for carrying liquids, whether water, wine, or milk. It was a skin bottle of this character that Abraham gave to Hagar when she was banished into the wilderness (Gen. xxi. 15, 19). These skin bottles were also employed to contain milk, and in them the milk was churned. In *Picturesque Palestine* (div. vi. p. 48) we have a vivid illustration of the process. To the corners of the skin bottle, filled with milk, cords are tied, and the skin is thus suspended from three sticks, which are inclined so as to meet at a point above. A girl is sitting beneath, and is swaying the suspended bottle to and fro.

We also read in the Old Testament of the use of *baskets*, and the original language shows that the ancient Hebrews possessed at least *four* different kinds. The *sal* was made from twigs or osiers, and was chiefly used for carrying bread (Gen. xl. 17, Exod. xxix. 3, 23, etc.). It probably resembled the modern Arabic equivalent of the same name, as well as the *kaneon* of the Greeks, or *canistrum* of the Romans (Verg., *Æneid*, viii. 180). It might even contain flesh (Judg. vi. 19). We come next to the *tĕnĕ*, mentioned in Deuteronomy xxvi. 2, 4 as the basket in which the firstfruits were placed and conveyed to the temple. From the rendering of this word in the LXX, we may infer that it was a basket which tapers downwards. We know from the oracle in Amos (viii. 1, 2) that the *clûb* was used for carrying summer fruit. On the other hand a *fourth* variety, called the *dûd*, was of larger size than either of the preceding, and was employed for carrying heavy weights, as we may infer from the language of Psalm lxxxi. 6, in which freedom from burdens is spoken of.[1]

From baskets we pass, by an easy transition, to pots. And here again we notice that the Hebrew language is rich in the variety of its names for these objects, and from this we conclude that this diversity of *name* indicates considerable diversity of *form* in the object designated. Besides the 'pot' (*parûr*), or ordinary vessel used to contain, for example, broth (Judg. vi. 19), or for boiling the manna (Num. xi. 8), we meet with the *sîr*, a large vessel or pan chiefly employed in cooking flesh, and hence associated with flesh in Exodus xvi. 3. That it was a pan or open vessel of considerable size is evident from the fact that it was also employed for washing. It is this word that is rendered 'wash-pot' in Psalm lx. 8. It must be distinguished from the *kiyyôr*, which was also used for washing (Exod. xxx. 18, xxxi. 9; 1 Kings vii. 38, 40, 43), and is rendered 'laver,' and was made of bronze, whereas the *sîr* was probably of earthenware. From Zechariah xii. 6, we learn that the *kiyyôr* also signified a brazier to contain fire. There is no evidence that it was employed for cooking. The growth of the Hebrew race in civilization is indicated

---

[1] This word (*dûd*) is also employed to express a kettle or pot, a meaning which belongs to the corresponding word in Aramaic (1 Sam. ii. 14; Job xli. 11; 2 Chron. xxxv. 13).

by the number of different words existing in the language for 'basin' or 'bowl.' These we have not space to characterize in detail, nor is it easy to distinguish one from the other. The *saph* meant a basin or bowl. In Exodus xii. 22 it is used to contain the blood with which the doorposts were sprinkled. On the other hand, the *mizrak* appears to have been a basin of larger size, though employed for a like purpose. Both the *kiyyôr* and the *saph* are terms that designate vessels employed in religious ritual. A list of such words may be found in Exodus xxxviii. 3; 1 Kings vii. 50; Jeremiah lii. 18, 19 (2 Kings xxiv. 14, 15). The word *mizrak*, however, was used in preexilian times to signify a mixing bowl (Amos vi. 6), into which the wine was emptied from the wine skin. Contrasted with this large mixing bowl (Lat. *crater*) was the wine cup (*kôs*), which was replenished from the former.

CHAPTER II

OUTDOOR LIFE AND OCCUPATIONS

13. WE now pass from the household to consider the **outdoor occupations** of ancient Israel. All the indications of the Old Testament clearly show that primitive Israel was a nomadic and *pastoral* people. And among certain tribes, especially Judah, inhabiting the southern and less fertile portion of Palestine, as well as Reuben and Gad, upon the eastern side of the Jordan, pastoral life undoubtedly prevailed very largely for several centuries after the death of Joshua. Thus, in what is generally held to be one of the earliest songs of Israel, Dehorah rebukes the tribe of Reuben with the words:

> 'Why didst thou stay among the sheep pens,
> Hearing the pipings of the flocks?'

And when we examine the references to the earlier period of Israel's history, these indications multiply. Let the following passages suffice: Gen. xii. 16, xiii. 5, xx. 14, xxi. 27, xxiv. 35, xxxii. 5, xxxiv. 28, xlvii. 17; Exod. x. 9, 24. And this condition of pastoral life Israel shared with the surrounding peoples, *e.g.* the Bedouin of the Sinaitic peninsula in the time of Moses (Exod. iii. 1), the Canaanites in the time of Joshua (Josh. vi. 21), the Philistines and the Amalekites in the time of Saul (1 Sam. xiv. 32, xv. 21). In the instances last cited the fact that flocks and herds were taken as spoil by the conquering Israelites indicates that both conquerors and conquered were to a certain extent pastoral in their occupations. Moab remained a pastoral country during the regal period. In the time of Jehoram, King of Israel, it sent him the wool of 100,000 lambs and 100,000 rams as tribute (2 Kings iii. 4; comp. Isaiah xvi. 1). Central and Southern Palestine must have been largely nomadic in the time of Saul and David. Nabal kept 3,000 sheep and 1,000 goats upon the slopes of Mount Carmel. Indeed, this continued for centuries to be a well-known pasture for flocks and herds (Mic. vii. 14). So also Bashan (Deut. xxxii. 14; Ezek. xxxix. 18), Sharon (Isa. lxv. 10), and Gilead (Micah vii. 14). From Amos vii. 1 and 1 Chronicles xxvii. 31 we learn that the kings of Israel were possessors of flocks and herds. Sheep were frequently tended by the daughters of the owners (Gen. xxix. 9; Exod. ii. 16), or by the sons (1 Sam. xvi. 11, xvii. 15). Human affection for animals is often exhibited in the traits of ancient Oriental life. Of this we have a vivid example in the parable of Nathan (2 Sam. xii. 1–4), with its pathetic story of the poor man who had an ewe lamb reared up with his own children : 'It did eat of his own morsel, and drank of his own cup, and lay in his bosom, and was unto him as a daughter.' In this connection it is to be noted that the name *Rachel*[1] in

---

[1] W. R. Smith, *Kinship and Marriage*, p. 219; Benzinger, *Hebrew Archæology*, p. 152. Some of these proper names point back in origin to animal totems.

Hebrew signifies an *ewe*. A like meaning belongs to the proper name of endearment, *Talitha*. Shepherds frequently called the wethers of the flock, and probably others besides, by special names (John x. 3).

Throughout the summer the sheep pastured in the open air by day, and by night were gathered into pens and carefully counted (Jer. xxxiii. 13). These pens or folds are called in Arabic at the present time *jedarah*, the same word in reality as the corresponding Hebrew term used in Numbers xxxii. 16, 24, 36: 'The common sheepfolds of Palestine are to this day large enclosures formed of the jedars,'[1] or rude stone fences for gardens, to be presently described. That sheep dogs were employed by the ancient Hebrews is clearly shown by Job xxx. 1.

The dress and accoutrements of the shepherd may be best illustrated from the description by the Rev. James Neil, of a modern representative.[2] 'The Syrian shepherd has two implements of his calling, neither of which is wanting when he is on full duty. His dress consists of a *kamise* or unbleached calico shirt, gathered in round the waist by a strong red leather belt. Hung to this belt, the leathern girdle of Scripture, which all workmen and labourers wear, besides his rude clasp knife and small leather pouch or " scrip," is a formidable weapon of defence, a short bludgeon, used to protect himself and his charge from assailants. It is generally made of a species of oak that is to be found in fine park-like groves on the highlands of Gilead and Bashan. It is about two feet long, and often has a large number of heavy iron nails

---

[1] Neil, *Palestine Explored*, p. 53.
[2] *Ibid.*, p. 255 foll.

driven into its round head,' thus rendering it a very deadly weapon. 'This club [called in Hebrew *shêbhet*] is easily attached to the belt, being furnished with a noose or cord passed through a hole in the end by which it is grasped.'[1] 'The guardian of the flock also carries a long shepherd's *staff* [called in Hebrew *mish'ân*, because is was used as a stay or support]. Its use answers to that of the shepherd's crook, viz. to guide the sheep, to rescue them from danger, to rule the stragglers into order, and at times to chastise the wilful.' Another use is indicated by a passage in the Korân (xx. 19), which refers to it in the words, 'It is the staff on which I lean, and with which I *beat down leaves for my sheep*.'[2] These remarks illustrate the well-known passage in Psalm xxiii., where the poet, addressing Jehovah, the Divine Shepherd, says: 'Thy club and Thy staff—they shall comfort me' (comp. Mic. vii. 14). The same word for club (*shêbhet*) also meets us in Psalm ii. 9 (comp. Num. xxiv. 17), where the poet describes Jehovah as clothing the anointed king with authority, so that he shall break in pieces his foreign foes with an *iron mace*. It is noticeable that in both Assyrian and Hebrew a ruler is often designated by the word 'shepherd' (comp. 2 Sam. v. 2, vii. 7; Jer. xxiii. 1 foll.). Sargon, in one of his inscriptions, calls himself 'faithful shepherd.' This phrase is evidently derived from the early primitive times, when the Semitic tribes were pastoral.

Numerous indications in the Old Testament clearly reveal the arduous nature of a herdsman's duties.

---

[1] Neil, *Palestine Explored*, p. 262.
[2] Cited by Prof. Cheyne in his comment on Psalm xxiii.

'In the day,' says Jacob to Laban, 'the drought consumed me, and the frost by night, and my sleep fled from my eyes.' According to the custom in early Israel, described in the brief compend of its legislation (Exod. xx. 22–xxiii.), the servant was guaranteed against liability to compensate his master for losses in the flocks, for which he as herdsman was not responsible. Laban, however, extorted more than his legal rights (Gen. xxxi. 39). In addition to the ordinary hardships were the perils from robber bands (*ibid.*, 1 Sam. xxx. 20; Job i. 17), and from wild beasts (1 Sam. xvii. 34, 35).

Respecting *goats*, which constitute a considerable and important part [1] of the small cattle, little need be said. Their milk was greatly esteemed (Prov. xxvii. 27), and was reputed to be more wholesome than that of sheep. The flesh of the goat and of the kid were highly valued as food, and hence both were offered in sacrifice (Judg. vi. 19). The flesh of the kid was considered a special delicacy, and was served in honour of guests (Judg. xiii. 15), and was, therefore, selected by Rebekah as a savoury dish for Isaac (Gen. xxvii. 9). At the present day the custom differs. In Syria the flesh of the sheep is the usual delicacy, while the poorer inhabitants have to content themselves with that of the kid (Benzinger).

14. The entrance of the **nomadic tribes** of Israel into the highlands and valleys of Palestine, already occupied by a group of races some of whom were more highly civilized than the Hebrews, was productive of a great change in habits and modes of life, which even extended to the religious usages of the

---

[1] 1 Sam. xxv. 2; Song of Sol. vi. 5; Prov. xxvii. 26.

conquering sons of Jacob. In the opening five chapters of the Book of Judges we clearly see the gradual process by which Israel's conquest of and extensions in Canaan were achieved. Probably the settlement of the Hebrew tribes was accomplished quite as much by peaceful as by warlike methods, though in the annals of the Hebrew, as of all other peoples, the military episodes obtain great prominence, and quite overshadowed the no less important and certain processes of peaceful intercourse. But an instructive passage (Deut. vi. 10-15) shows us how potent the latter influences were in moulding the civilization of God's chosen race. Israel in truth must have received far more than he gave. When we turn to that primitive compend of laws, the Book of the Covenant (Exod. xxi.–xxiii.), we see the legislation of a society 'of a very simple structure.' A distinguished Old Testament scholar and Arabist has observed that its principles of civil and criminal justice are those still current among the Arabs of the desert. These traditions of Israel's early nomadic life are still maintained. But a remarkable change is manifest. The stage of civilization which is contemplated in the legislation is not so much nomadic or pastoral as *agricultural*. We notice, for example, the prominence that is given to the *ox* among the animals domesticated to man's use (Exod. xxi. 28, xxii. 13 *passim*), since it was the ox that was employed for ploughing (1 Sam. xiv. 14; 1 Kings xix. 19; Amos vi. 12; Job i. 14; Deut. xxii. 10), and also for treading out or threshing the corn (Hos. x. 11; Mic. iv. 13; Deut. xxv. 4). The *ass* is usually conjoined with the ox in the enumerations of cattle (Exod. xx. 17, xxii. 9).

We know that this animal was likewise employed in ploughing (Deut. xxii. 10), and still more in riding (Num. xxii. 21 foll.; 1 Sam. xxv. 20 foll.; 2 Kings iv. 24; Zech. ix. 9). For in the golden days of Hebrew nationality the *horse* was not employed in peaceful avocations. It was foreign, like the chariot, and its use was deprecated as such in prophecy and law (Hos. xiv. 3; Deut. xvii. 16; comp. Pss. xx. 7, xxxiii. 17). Egypt was the market whence horses were exported to other nations. From 1 Kings x. 28 we learn that Solomon imported his war horses from this region, and more than two centuries later we find the great Assyrian conqueror, Sargon, in his triumphal inscription, referring to the Egyptian steeds which came into his possession (Khorsab., line 183). Trusting in horses, or in the chariots to which they were yoked, was regarded as a departure from the primitive simplicity of Israel's life, and an act of reliance upon foreign aids. In the Deuteronomic legislation such conduct was construed as an act of disloyalty to Jehovah. Royal personages or men of distinction would therefore avoid riding on horseback. If not content with the lowly ass (Matt. xxi. 7; Zech. ix. 9), they rode upon the more stately *mule* (2 Sam. xiii. 29, xviii. 9; 1 Kings i. 33).

15. **Agriculture**, then, is the chief basis of ancient Hebrew life presupposed in the Book of the Covenant. Of this we have already given one clear indication. Another consists in the religious festivals, three in number, to which reference is made in the earliest code of legislation (Exod. xxiii. 14 foll.). These feasts were obviously regulated by the harvesting operations of the dwellers in Canaan,

Palestine, with the exception of the southernmost portion, was a fairly well-watered region of mountains and valleys (Deut. viii. 7–9), and stood in this respect contrasted with Egypt (Deut. xi. 10–12), with its vast plains irrigated from the Nile overflow. In the current phraseology of the ancient Hebrew, it 'flowed with milk and honey.' In those days the land was more fruitful than it has been since the wars of the Assyrians, Babylonians, Persians, and all the different subsequent waves of conquest which laid the country waste and deprived it of trees. Isaiah's oracles make reference to the destruction of timber by the Assyrian invaders (ii. 13, ix. 10, (9 Heb.), x. 33).[1] The 'early rain' begins in October. It is not continuous, but intermittent, and thus enables the cultivator to sow wheat and barley. It continues to fall at intervals during November and December, and even occurs as late as March and April (latter rain). All the remaining months till October there is cloudless weather.

As soon as the ground in October has been softened by showers, the sowing of the wheat, barley and lentils begins. The plough of the ancient Hebrew probably resembled its modern counterpart very closely. Taking the plough of the modern fellaheen of Palestine as our model, it may be briefly described as consisting of a pole made up of two pieces, to which a cross-piece was fastened to which the oxen were attached. At the other end a piece was inserted at

[1] Esarhaddon, in his inscriptions, reports that he received cedar and cyprus wood as tribute, while Asurbanipal states that he employed planks of cedar from Sirion and Lebanon for the erection of his palace. Tiglath Pileser's inscriptions allude to the destruction of an enemy's palm groves.

an obtuse angle, terminating in the share at the lower end and a rude sort of handle at the upper. With this rude instrument the surface of the ground was loosened, the share hardly penetrating more than four or five inches below the surface. The oxen were driven with a goad called *malmâd*, furnished with an iron point, so as to form an excellent substitute for a spear which Shamgar wielded with deadly effect (Judg. iii. 31; comp. 1 Sam. xiii. 21), but was employed by the ploughman not only for goading the oxen (comp. Acts ix. 5), but for breaking up the clods or clearing the plough. An interesting though difficult passage in Isaiah (xxviii. 24, 25) clearly shows that the three processes whereby the ground was prepared for the seed consisted of ploughing, then breaking up the clods by harrowing, and lastly levelling the surface. From Matthew xiii. 3-8 we may infer that the seed was then sown broadcast, as is represented on the Egyptian monuments, some of outermost grains being even scattered on the wayside which bordered on the field. In the ancient Egyptian representations we see vividly portrayed the sower immediately following the plough. In his left hand there is held a basket of seed, while his right is left free for scattering the seed.

It is impossible to say whether the Hebrews understood the principle of rotation of crops. They entertained scruples about sowing a field with different seeds (Deut. xxii. 9), and from early times they regarded it as a sacred duty to let the land remain fallow in the Sabbatic or seventh year (Exod. xxiii. 10, 11).

Harvest commences at the end of March or begin-

MODERN PLOUGH AND PEASANT.

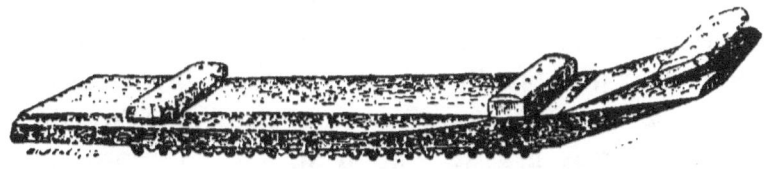

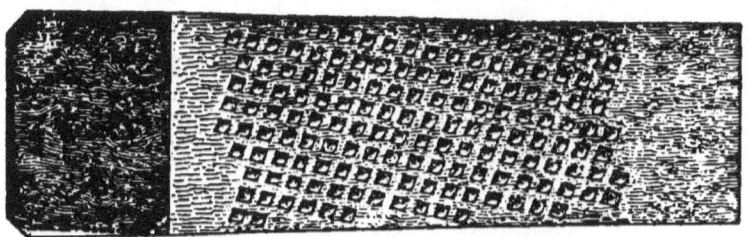

MODERN THRESHING SLEDGES.

ning of April. In the lower or warmer portion of Palestine and in the valley of the Jordan it begins at the end of March. The *barley* harvest came first, and that of *wheat* came last (middle of May). The entire harvesting of the corn occupied seven weeks, and was a period of joyful labour, which found expression in the religious festival of the month *Sivan*, called the Feast of Weeks or Pentecost. The gladness which characterized this season in the year's agricultural calendar became proverbial among the ancient Hebrews. Thus Isaiah, in describing the prosperity and joy of the coming Messianic Ruler, says, 'They rejoice before Thee like the joy in harvest' (Isa. ix. 3; Heb. 2). The weather at this time was almost always fine, and the occurrence of thunderstorms was so unusual that it was regarded in the light of a Divine visitation (1 Sam. xii. 17; comp. Prov. xxvi. 1).

The corn was reaped by a sickle, called by the Hebrews *chermēsh* or *maggâl* (the Arabic *minjâl*). Sometimes the corn may have been pulled up by the roots, as is the practice at the present day in Egypt when barley or *dourra* is being reaped. Probably the sickle was usually employed, and the corn was cut fairly *low*, as the dream of Joseph, in which the sheaves are described as *bowing* to the earth, would seem to imply. Also the phrase occurring in Isaiah (xvii. 5), 'his arm reapeth the ears,' would appear to indicate this.

The most vivid picture of the harvest fields of ancient days may be found in the Book of Ruth. Vessels of water were provided for the refreshment of the reapers (Ruth ii. 9). Morsels of bread were dipped in vinegar and eaten; also parched corn

EGYPTIAN HARVEST OPERATIONS.
(*Relief from the tomb of Ti in Sakkara.*)

1. Storing the sheaves.   2. Oxen and asses treading the corn.   3. Women and men winnowing the corn.

(*kali*) was provided, a favourite diet with workers who led an outdoor life[1] (Ruth ii. 14). Some of these details are illustrated by the Egyptian monuments, in which we find representations of water skins hung up on trees in the harvest field, while pitchers are standing close by, to be replenished by the thirsty reapers, some of whom are seen already applying them to their lips. The merciful provision of the Deuteronomic code provided that the remnants of the sheaves that were not carried off on carts from the field (Amos ii. 13) should be left for the benefit of the alien sojourner, the fatherless or the widow. In the even greater generosity of the Levitical code (Lev. xix. 9) the corners of the field were specially reserved for this charitable purpose (Ruth ii. 7, 8).

The stalks were gathered into sheaves or heaps and conveyed to a floor consisting of a circular piece of ground some twenty yards across and exposed to the wind, and here oxen or asses were driven over the floor over which the corn had been spread, and the grains by this process of treading were freed from the husks. These threshingfloors became permanent, and were named after the original owners. Thus we read of the threshingfloor of Nachon (or, according to the Chronicler, Chidon) and the threshingfloor of Araunah (2 Sam. vi. 6, xxiv. 18). The oxen were sometimes driven two or more abreast, at other times indiscriminately over the floor. An interesting trait of ancient Hebrew life shows that kindly consideration for the welfare of the beast characterized these early times (comp. Prov. xii. 10), and this was the merciful

---

[1] *Kali* or roast corn was sent as provision for soldiers during a campaign (1 Sam. xvii. 17 ; 2 Sam. xvii. 28).

provision that the ox should not be muzzled when treading out the corn which he was thus preparing for the use of man, but should be permitted to eat some share of the grain (Deut. xxv. 4).

Other means were also adopted beside this rough and ready method of separating the grains from the husk. Among these was a staff or rude flail, for beating out small portions of corn (Isa. xxviii. 27); but more frequently the instrument employed was the *môrag* (also called *charûts*) or 'threshing sledge,' corresponding to the ancient Italian *tribulum*, a plank fitted with sharp-pointed stones, which were fixed into holes in the bottom. This was drawn by the oxen over the corn (Isa. xxviii. 27), the driver often sitting on the sledge to increase the weight. Another variety of the threshing sledge consisted of a small framework upon wheels, sharp iron blades being attached to the wheels, so as to cut through the corn. Hence the prophets used the powerful metaphor of the threshing sledge to describe the cruel treatment of a conquered people (Amos i. 3; comp. 2 Kings xiii. 7).

Then followed the process of winnowing. The bruised corn was thrown up upon wooden shovels when a moderate breeze was blowing. The wind carried away the chaff from the threshingfloor, while the heavier grains remained behind. Only a moderate steady wind availed for this purpose. Thus Jeremiah, in his lamentation over his degenerate countrymen, makes use of this metaphor, 'a vehement wind from the bare heights in the wilderness is the way of my people; 'tis not for winnowing or for cleansing' (Jer. iv. 11). Wetzstein, in one of his useful notes contributed to Delitzsch's Commentary on Job, tells us that it is only when the wind blows from the west or south the moderate breeze suitable for winnowing is obtained; the north wind is too violent, while the east wind blows in constant gusts, which carry away grains as well as chaff.

Beside the winnowing there was also the 'cleansing,' as the above passage indicates. The latter was rendered absolutely necessary on account of the rough and ready process of treading out the corn described above. Not only was the corn shaken to and fro in a *sieve* (*kebârah*)—a process to which Amos makes vivid reference in a metaphor (Amos ix. 9),—but it was needful to clear the wheat carefully of stones or dirt, which became mixed up with it. This duty, like many others, frequently fell to the lot of women. Of this we have an interesting illustration preserved to us in the Septuagint version of 2 Samuel iv. 6, which enables us to restore what is probably the original text. We there learn that the two assassins who slew Ishbosheth were able to enter his house at noon unobserved because the woman who acted as portress at the entrance had fallen asleep over the task of cleansing wheat (see Driver's notes on the Hebrew Text of the Books of Samuel *ad loc*).

Long straw was not valued by the ancient Hebrews as with us, but the short, chopped straw (called *tébhen*) was used as food for oxen (Isa. xi. 7). It was customary in Palestine in those days to store up the corn (as well as oil or honey) in subterranean chambers (Jer. xli. 8), and, according to Robinson, the custom still survives.

The great extent of corn cultivation in Palestine from the time of Solomon downwards is evident from innumerable indications in the Old Testament. Two of the three ancient religious festivals of Canaan—the Feast of Unleavened Cakes and the Feast of Weeks or Harvest—were based upon the operations of the corn harvest, which played so large a part in the life of the agricultural community. The old name for the first month of the ecclesiastical year was not *Nisan* (which is Babylonian) but *Abib*, which in ancient Hebrew meant ears of corn. Palestine, in fact, was, as the Book of Deuteronomy continually reminds us, a great corn-producing as well as wine-and-olive-producing country. When Hiram, King of Tyre, came to visit Solomon, the Phœnician king was supplied by the Hebrew monarch with 20,000 measures of wheat for food for his household, and twenty measures of pure oil (1 Kings v. 11). This fact is significant because it exhibits the close economic relation which subsisted between the wealthy emporia of commerce of that Northern maritime race and the fertile valleys and plains of Canaan. It shows us the commercial basis of advantage that prompted the dynastic alliance between the house of Omri and that of Ethbaal, of Sidon, cemented by the marriage of Ahab and Jezebel. There can be little doubt that the wealth that poured into Israel in the days of Isaiah, to which he makes reference (Isa. ii. 7; comp. iii. 18 foll., as well as Amos iii. 15, vi. 4 foll.), came from the great ports of Tyre and Sidon, where the merchandise of all nations, from Spain to India, was gathered together. So close indeed was this link of connection between Phœnicia and Israel that Amos calls it a 'covenant of brethren' (Amos i. 9). In exchange for the 'silver and the gold' and articles of luxury, Israel supplied the Phœnician markets with stores of grain. This relation subsisted for centuries. In Ezekiel's minute description of the greatness of Tyre he mentions (xxvii. 17), Minnith wheat, oil and honey among the chief articles imported from Judah in his own time (6th century B.C.). More than six centuries later we still find that Canaan supplied Phœnicia with corn, for a special deputation came (about 44 A.D.) to King Herod Agrippa from Tyre and Sidon, 'asking for peace, because their country was fed from the king's country' (Acts xii. 20).

16. Perhaps the next most important growth of the Canaanite agriculture was the *vine* (comp. Deut. xxxiii. 28). Its ancient origin is attested by the story of Noah (Gen. ix. 20, 21), as well as the names of places in ancient Canaan. Thus the name of the valley '*Eshcol*' or 'cluster,' and the name of the Philistine town *Gath*[1] or 'winepress'; Beth-hakkerem, 'house of the vine' (Jer. vi. 1; Neh. iii. 14), show the prevailing occupations of the people in ancient times. Several names of places are compounded of the element *Gath*. The cultivation of the vine and the olive is distinguished above that of cereals, in requiring years of patient and assiduous labour before adequate results are obtained. Here again the parabolic language of prophecy affords us a clear insight into these facts of every-day life. In Isaiah's pathetic oracle of the degenerate vine (chap. v.) he describes the patient toil bestowed by the Divine Husbandman in the preparation of the

---

[1] There were several places into which this prefix of *Gath* or winepress entered. Thus there was a Gath-Hepher in Zebulun (Josh. xix. 13), and there was likewise a Gath-Rimmon.

ground. A mountain side is selected possessed with a rich soil, and as in this case a plough could not possibly be used on its steep sides, it was worked over with a mattock or hoe (called by the Arabs *miz'ak*). This was done two or three times a year, the ground being carefully cleared of stones. It was also necessary on the slope of a hill to form the land into terraces, well banked up and protected so as to prevent the winter rains from carrying away the soil. The same passage in Isaiah also refers to the watch tower erected in the midst of vineyards as well as of other fruit or vegetable gardens,[1] to serve as a shelter for the watchmen who guarded the vineyard from depredations by robbers. Thus, in a parallel passage to that which we are now considering, Isaiah recites a brief lay, called 'the pleasant vineyard' (xxvii. 2 foll.).

> 'I Jehovah am its keeper,
> Every moment I am watering it.
> Lest one make a raid upon it,
> Night and day am I watching it.'

There was another means of protection, viz., walls or hedges, to keep out the incursions of wild animals, and the predatory hands of man. Thus, in the beautiful eightieth Psalm, with its elegant strophic arrangement, the poet refers to the mournful condition of Israel towards the close of the reign of Hoshea (or perhaps of his predecessor, Pekah), when the Northern kingdom was at the mercy of the Assyrian. Appeal-

---

[1] In ordinary orchards and gardens there was frequently nothing more than a booth or hut for this purpose, as in the vineyard and the cucumber field of Isaiah i. 8.

ing to Jehovah, who had brought Israel as a vine out of Egypt, the psalmist exclaims (12 foll.) :—

'Why hast thou broken down its fences,
And all who pass by on the way pluck [its fruit]?
The wild boar from the forest gnaws it,
And the roving beast of the field feeds on it.
O God of hosts, pray look down again from heaven,
See and visit this vine.'

These stone fences have been already mentioned in connection with sheep pens. They form so characteristic an element of the country life of ancient as well as modern Palestine that we borrow once more from the graphic pen of the Rev. James Neil : 'Throughout Palestine gardens, orchards, and vineyards, unlike other cultivated spots, are always enclosed.' This rude wall of rough, unhewn stones, of all sizes, is called in Arabic a *jedar*, which is the same word as the word for 'wall' or 'fence' in Hebrew (*gadēr*), occurring in the above psalm. 'The ground is first smoothed, and the stones are then piled up, about three feet in width at the bottom and gradually narrowing towards the top. No mortar of any kind is employed, the stones being merely laid so as to fit closely together.' The height varies from four or six to even twelve feet, but the whole structure is rather frail. 'In some ways this is an advantage, for a thief, whether man or beast, cannot easily climb over it without throwing down the loose stones, and so giving notice of his approach. The heavy rain-storms of winter constantly bring down portions of the *jedars* by undermining the soft foundation of earth.' We are now enabled to realize more vividly the scene of Balaam's vision, when he beheld the angel of Jehovah standing 'in the depressed gully between vineyards, a wall (*gadēr*) on one side and a wall on the other' (Num. xxii. 24). 'Vividly it recalls to my mind places where I have had to pass through similar narrow passages, only a few feet across, separating the massive vineyard hedges of rough, unhewn stone. These loose, unmortared walls afford endless hot, dusty crevices, in which the serpent tribe delight. They can, moreover, be easily thrown down by any mischievously disposed person.' This enables us to understand the force of the saying in Ecclesiastes x. 8, 'Whosoever breaketh down a wall (*gadēr*), a serpent bites him' (*Palestine Explored*, p. 54).

The best kind of vine is called in Hebrew *sorēk* (or *sorēkah*), and it is this finer quality of vine the Divine Husbandman is described by Isaiah in his poem as planting on the fertile mountain side. Vines were sometimes allowed to spread along the ground (Isa. xvi. 8; Ezek. xvii. 6, xix. 10), and sometimes were trained upon poles or upon trees, as, for example, cedars, Psalm lxxx. 10 (just as among the Italians they were 'married' to elm trees. Vergil, *Georg.*, i. 2, ii. 361). Dr. Robinson has described the appearance of vines in Southern Palestine (*Biblical Researches*, ii. 80 foll.) : 'They are planted singly in rows eight or ten feet apart in each direction. The stock is suffered to grow up large to the height of six or eight feet, and is then fastened in a sloping position to a strong stake, and the shoots suffered to grow from one plant to another, forming a line of festoons. Sometimes two rows are made to slant towards each other, and thus form by their shoots a sort of arch. These shoots are pruned away in autumn. (Comp. John xv. 2.)

The enormous size of the bunches of grapes discovered by the spies in the valley of Eshcol (Num. xiii. 23) is fully confirmed by the testimony of modern travellers in Palestine. One German traveller asserts that he has himself seen clusters that weigh ten or twelve pounds.

Beside the provisions for the safety of the vineyard, it was also endowed with a winepress and a winevat. The *winepress* (called *Gath* or *Purah*) is described by Isaiah (in the song of God's vineyard) as being cut out as a trough in the solid rock. Beneath it, and communicating with the trough or winepress above by a hole, another and smaller chamber was excavated, which was the *wine-vat*, called in Hebrew *yekebh*. Robinson, in his great work (*Biblical Researches*, vol. iii. pp. 137, 603), describes them as still remaining in Palestine. The upper or more shallow trough would be about eight feet square and fifteen inches deep, while the lower vat (*yekebh*) would be about four feet square and about three feet deep. The ripe grapes were gathered in baskets (Jer. vi. 9, LXX. and Vulg.; Amos viii. 2), and were cast in heaps into the winepress. The prevailing colour of the grapes of ancient days was undoubtedly purple, since the juice of the grape is constantly compared to blood. Thus when the grapes were trod in the winepress their juice spurted over the garments of those who trod, and dyed them with blood-red colour, a circumstance to which Hebrew poets frequently alluded. In the blessing of Jacob the prosperity

Judah is portrayed in graphic touches. He is described as—

> 'Binding his young ass to the vine,
> And his ass's foal to the *sorēk*
> He washed in blood his garments,
> And in the blood of grapes his clothing.'

And with still more dramatic effect does the prophet represent the conqueror of Edom, Israel's age-long foe (Isa. lxiii. 2 foll.), whom he challenges with the question :—

> 'Why is there redness in thy apparel,[1]
> And thy garments like that of a treader of the winepress?'

To which the victor replies :—

> 'The wine trough have I trodden by myself,
> And there was no man of the nations with me ;
> So I was treading them in my anger,
> And was trampling on them in my wrath ;
> And their life-juice bespattered my garments,
> And all my clothing I stained.'

The grape juice which flowed into the vat or *yekebh* below was then collected in vessels. In its unfermented condition as 'must' it was called by the Hebrews *tîrôsh*, or new wine, and drunk in this condition. On the other hand, the fermented wine was called by a variety of names, which need not here be detailed.

The vintage period in Palestine is the month of September, but the grapes begin to ripen even in June. The whole process of the gathering of the grapes and the treading of the winepress, while the juice poured forth into the foaming vats, formed one

---

[1] Or perhaps we ought to read with LXX., 'Why is thy apparel red?'

of the most characteristic elements of the free, ancient Canaanite life. Like the operations of the corn harvest, it found expression in one of the three agricultural festivals, called the Feast of 'Booths' (originally Feast of 'Ingathering'). This feast was common to Canaanites and Hebrews alike, as the reader can clearly see from Judges ix. 27. It was a time of universal merrymaking and joy, when the shout of 'them that tread the grapes' (Jer. xxv. 30) could be heard among the vineyards. Hence Isaiah or some earlier prophet, when denouncing doom against the fruitful regions of Moab, exclaims: 'Gladness is banished and joy out of the fruitful field, and in the vineyards there shall be no song nor joyous noise; no treader shall tread out wine in the presses' (Isa. xvi. 10).

It was an ancient custom to pay the firstfruits of corn, wine and oil to Jehovah as Lord of the land, or, in other words, to the priesthood (Exod. xxii. 29; Deut. xviii. 4; Neh. x. 37), and we may probably gather from Hosea ix. 1 and other indications that this was the practice of the Canaanites also in their worship of Baal. Vineyards, like cornfields and olive yards, enjoyed a Sabbatic year of rest, *i.e.* lay fallow every seventh year (Exod. xxiii. 11; Lev. xxv. 3 foll.). Moreover, the strongest scruples were felt against sowing a vineyard with different seeds. This found expression in the legislation of Deuteronomy xxii. 9, which threatened complete confiscation of the produce by the priesthood (as the language evidently implies).[1] As in the corn harvest, so in the vintage,

---

[1] Comp. Leviticus xix. 19, where the same objection is ex-

special provision was made for the wants of the destitute. The alien, the fatherless and widow, were to glean the remaining bunches that were left behind by the grape gatherers (Deut. xxiv. 21 ; Lev. xix. 10).

The wine was drawn off from the vats into jars, and more frequently into wineskins. They were then left alone for the wine to ferment. Now and then the wine was left to stand in the jars for some time before it was poured off into other vessels (comp. Jer. xlviii. 11, 12). The object of this was that the wine, after the process of fermentation, might gain in richness of flavour as well as colour. When it had been carefully purified through a strainer, it was esteemed a very choice delicacy—the 'wine on the lees well refined' of Isaiah's prophecy, in which God is described as preparing a 'feast of fat things' upon Mount Zion for all peoples (Isa. xxv. 6).

Grapes were also dried to make *raisins* (called in Hebrew *tzimmûk*), just as is done in Palestine at the present day. These were pressed into a solid cake, so as to be easily conveyed from place to place. So also the dried figs. They were much used in ancient Israel, as well as the parched corn (*kali*), by troops on the march (1 Sam. xxv. 18, xxx. 12). Moreover, the

---

pressed against clothing of different materials (also in Deut. xxii. 11). When we take these special statutes in connection with the entire group of laws in Leviticus and in Deuteronomy among which they stand, they must be held to express Divine disapprobation of hybrids. Intermarriage, even among different clans of the same race, was exceptional among the Hebrews, as already explained. It appears to have been considered to be God's purpose to keep every object He has made pure and distinct, as He originally made it. Intermixture was man's travesty of God's workmanship. Compare Dillmann's Note on Leviticus xix. 19.

grape juice which came from the trodden clusters was 'boiled down to a syrup which, under the name of "honey" [Hebrew, *debâsh*; in modern Arabic, *dibs*], is much used by all classes in modern Palestine as a condiment with their food' (Robinson). It was exported from Palestine to Phœnicia, together with corn, as we learn from Ezekiel xxvii. 17. Not improbably the 'honey' mentioned among the gifts of Barzillai to David and his warriors (2 Sam. xvii. 29) means this.

The raisins were made into *raisin-cakes*, probably compounded with oil and flour, and so quite distinct from the *tzimmûk* mentioned above. These raisin-cakes were used in offerings, as Hosea iii. 1 clearly shows, and, as is usual with food-offerings, were also consumed by the faithful votaries. A cake of this kind is called *ashîshah*, and on the solemn and joyful occasion when the ark of God was brought into the city of David one of them was bestowed on each of the festive crowd (2 Sam. vi. 19).

That the Hebrews, like other peoples of antiquity, frequently drank to excess, and that their vintage festivals became scenes of drunken orgies, is obvious from many allusions in the Old Testament. This was rendered the more easy, not only by the fact that considerable portions of Palestine were a rich vine-growing country, but also from the close proximity of the more civilized and pleasure-loving Canaanites. The references in the prophetic oracles of the eighth century to the drinking banquets of the wealthier classes of the population are frequent. Amos vividly describes the revelry of those princes of Samaria who stretch themselves on beds of ivory, drinking 'wine in bowls, and anoint themselves with choicest unguents,' 'singing idle songs to the sound of the viol' (vi. 4-6). Indeed, to judge from the language of the prophets at this time, the inhabitants of the fertile land of Ephraim bore a very bad repute for their habits of intemperance. Hosea describes in one graphic touch how the nobles made themselves ill with the feverish glow of wine in their carousals upon the king's birthday (Hos. vii. 5). These practices they carried on despite the evil omens of a disordered state and the advancing armies of the Assyrian foe, and Isaiah exclaims (xxviii. 1): 'Woe to the proud crown of Ephraim's drunkards, and the fading bloom of his brilliant array, which is on the height of the fertile valley of those who are smitten with wine.'

But the orgies of the Southern capital were equally revolting, and the same prophet portrays the carousals that went on in many a wealthy man's symposium in Jerusalem, the scenes of revelry beginning in early morning and continuing till nightfall. 'Woe to those that rise up early pursuing strong drink, who tarry till late in the dusk, while wine inflames them. Lute and guitar, tambourine, flute and wine are their banquet, but the work of Jehovah they do not regard.'

17. Next in importance to vine-culture was the cultivation of the **olive**. This might easily be illustrated by copious references to it in the Old Testament and to its frequent employment in metaphor. A faithful servant of Jehovah whose life is prosperous compares himself to a green olive tree (Ps. lii. 8), while his children are called 'olive branches around his table' (Ps. cxxviii. 3). The reader may compare for himself Hosea xiv. 6 and Jeremiah xi. 16. 'Dip-

ping the foot in oil' was the poetic expression of prosperity (Deut. xxxiii. 24).

Like the vine, the olive required much labour and careful attention. Trenches or reservoirs for water were needed at no great distance, and it was necessary to plough up the soil under the trees once or twice every year. The trees grow to a great age, and are surrounded by mounds of earth to protect them; but they only attain a moderate height, twenty or thirty feet with gnarled and knotted stem. Olive gardens were planted on mountain sides, or at any rate in a dry soil and sunny situation. The olive tree does not bear on the average more frequently than once in two years a full crop. The oblong brown berries sometimes attain the size of a dove's egg, changing in colour from green to purple and black. They begin ripening as early as September, but the harvest does not take place till October, and lasts even till November. The berries are not taken when fully ripe, since the fully ripe berries yield an oil of inferior quality.[1] They were not picked, but *shaken* off, the olive tree being beaten (Deut. xxiv. 20). Hence the language of Isaiah, whose vivid metaphors from agricultural life have so frequently illustrated these pages. Describing the impending ruin of Syria and its chief towns, he turns to Israel, and refers to the small remnant of inhabitants that shall be left by Jehovah's mercy: 'gleanings shall be left, as at the striking of the olive tree, two or three berries above at the topmost point, four or five in the fruit tree's

---

[1] Thus the better quality or 'white' oil is called by Pliny *omphácium*, a Greek name meaning 'unripe.' 'Quanto maturior bacca, tanto pinguior succus minusque gratus.'

boughs.' According to the humane legislation of the Deuteronomic code, these leavings of the olive gleaner were reserved for the aliens, the widow and the fatherless (Deut. xxiv. 20).

The first olive oil was obtained not by pressing, but by pounding the berries in a mortar. They were then placed in baskets, and the oil flowed off. This oil was the purest and best, the 'beaten oil' of Exodus xxvii. 20, Leviticus xxiv. 2, prescribed for consumption in the light of the sanctuary ('tent of meeting'). It is apparently the same as the fresh or 'green oil' which was used as an unguent for the person, and to which the psalmist refers in Psalm xcii. 10 (11 Heb.).

Olive oil was also obtained, like the new wine or *must*, by simply treading in the oilpress. In fact, the same word *Gath* is employed for both wine and oilpress. It occurs in the name Gethsemane, which has this latter meaning. There was similarly an *oilvat* attached to the oilpress (Joel ii. 24), into which the oil flowed. The value of the oil produced in Palestine is attested by the fact that it was an article of export and of tribute. Thus we read in Hosea's oracles (xii. 1) that 'oil was carried to Egypt' in his days by the emissaries of the Northern kingdom, in order to win over the alliance and support of the Pharaoh (comp. 2 Chron. xxxii. 28). As with the corn, wine and wool, so in the case of the olive, first-fruits and tithes of it were paid to the sanctuary (Deut. xii. 17, xviii. 4; 2 Chron. xxxi. 5; Neh. x. 37, 39).

Some of the uses of olive oil have already been indicated, viz., the anointing of the person with fresh oil and the use of the 'beaten oil' for the temple lights. In the anointing of the person the unguent was specially applied to the hair of the head as well as the beard. It was customary for the guests before a banquet to anoint themselves, or that this service should be rendered to them by attendants (compare the passages Deut. xxviii. 40; 2 Sam. xiv. 2; Ps. xxiii. 5, xcii. 10, civ. 15; Mic. vi. 15; Luke vii. 46). This universal Eastern usage of anointing the person was a natural result of climatic conditions, the intensity of the heat causing an injurious and disagreeable excess of perspiration and irritability of the skin, which the use of oil or other fatty substances tends to counteract. It became therefore an indispensable preliminary upon all occasions of social etiquette (Ruth iii. 3; Ezek. xvi. 9) for women as well as men (Prov. xxvii. 9; Song of Songs i. 3). It was expressly neglected in times of mourning, this exceptional disuse being the significant token of grief.

The oil used in anointing the person, employed by the wealthier classes at banquets or on special occasions, as weddings (Ps. xlv. 7, 8 (8, 9, Heb.), consisted of a mixture of oil and aromatic spices, as myrrh nard and frankincense. The myrrh and the frankincense came, as an instructive passage in Ezekiel tells us (xxvii. 22; comp. Isa. lx. 6; Jer. vi. 20), from the Sabæan district of Arabia into the Phœnician market.[1] Olive oil compounded with such spices

---

[1] Comp. also 1 Kings x. 10. From Phœnicia they were exported in small alabaster vases, or *vasa unguentaria*. The Roman poet Tibullus sings of one who is *Syrio madefactus tempora nardo*, while his contemporary Horace says (*Od.*, ii. 11, 16), *Assyriaque nardo potamus uncti*, since Syria is nothing more than an abbreviation of Assyria, the latter name having been originally given to the Aramæan and Phœnician lands by the

would be that expensive variety of unguent in which the nobles of Samaria in the days of Amos indulged (vi. 6). The preparations of these costly mixtures gave rise to a special industry, viz., that of the '*perfumer*' (called 'apothecary' in the English version, Exod. xxx. 25, 35; Neh. iii. 8; Eccles. x. 1). From 1 Samuel viii. 13 we might infer that this art was practised chiefly by women among the Hebrews in pre-exilian times (comp. also Isa. iii. 17, 24). One of the '*alabaster boxes*' (more correctly alabaster *vases*) of this precious ointment, sealed up to preserve the fragrance, was broken and poured by a 'woman that was a sinner' (Luke vii. 37, 38) upon our Lord's head (or, according to St. Luke's narrative, 'the feet') when He was entertained at the house of Simon the Leper (Mark xiv. 3). According to the testimony of Mark xiv. 5, its value was over 300 denarii, or at least £10. Our Lord spoke of this touching act of devotion as an anointing of His body for burial (Mark xiv. 8), an allusion which will be explained hereafter.

Greeks in the latter part of the 8th or earlier part of the 7th century, when the Mediterranean border became practically annexed to Assyria. Nard, it should be observed, is not a Semitic but a Persian or a Sanscrit word, and came from India. The 'distant country' (Jer. vi. 20) from which the 'sweet cane' or calamus came, may perhaps be South Arabia, but it is difficult to decide from the obscure passage in Ezekiel xxvii. 19. It is interesting to note that the sweet cane or calamus (*Ḳanû*), together with cedar wood, formed the incense offering made to the gods on the mountain summit in the cuneiform Flood-legend, line 150 (Delitzsch). The fragrant *aloe wood* of Psalm xlv. 8 is undoubtedly of Indian origin. It may here be remarked that the reference in the Old Testament literature (Exod. xxx. 25, 35; Eccles. x. 1; Neh. iii. 8, etc.) to the art of the perfumer would seem to indicate that during the exilian and post-exilian period the art was largely carried on by *men*.

From this special use of olive oil in the social etiquette of life arose another which was official and religious. The king was *anointed* to his high office, and was therefore called in Hebrew *mashiach, i.e.* Messiah or 'anointed.' Every king was regarded as anointed of God to rule (1 Sam. ii. 10, 35, xii. 3, xvi. 6, etc.). The term then came to be applied *par excellence* to that ideal prince of David's lineage with which Isaiah's prophecies made his countrymen familiar—a prince hero clothed with Divine authority, who was to rule in righteousness (Isa. ix. 6, 7 (5, 6 Heb.), xi. 1-9). This type of conception in the fulness of time found its complete realization in Jesus, *the Christ*—the Divine Prince of Peace.

A similar initiatory rite was performed on priests, and even prophets (1 Kings xix. 16). The 'holy anointing oil' with which Aaron and his priests were consecrated to their holy office was compounded with fragrant spices in special proportions, about which minute directions are given in Exodus xxx. 23 foll. Nor was this anointing confined to persons, but was applied to the tent of meeting, the ark of testimony, and the varied vessels and paraphernalia of the sanctuary.

Another most important use of oil was *medicinal*. Wounds, weals, or sores were mollified with oil, pressed and bound up (Isa. i. 6; Luke x. 34), also the sick were anointed with it (James v. 14). The balm or balsam prepared in Gilead from the mastix tree and terebinth was also a well-known remedy (Gen. xxxvii. 25; Jer. viii. 22, xlvi. 11, li. 8), which was exported into Egypt.

Lastly, and perhaps most important of all, was the

use of olive oil in food. In cooking it seems to have taken the place of butter or animal fat. Probably the pancakes made from dough which Tamar boiled and made for Amnon were compounded with olive oil. This we might infer from the vegetable *food offerings* prescribed in the Levitical laws. The meal offering described in Leviticus ii. 1-3 consisted of fine flour, oil and frankincense. Other meal offerings of a somewhat similar character, consisting of cakes made of wheaten flour and oil, are described in Exodus xxix. 2; Leviticus ii. 4 foll., vi. 20, 21, vii. 12, xiv. 10; Numbers vi. 15. The custom of sprinkling and *anointing the leper* with oil (Lev. xiv. 15 foll.), described with considerable minuteness, must be regarded as an act of ritual cleansing or consecrating, analogous to the use of the holy anointing oil, to which we have already referred. Perhaps, however, it may be regarded as a combination of medicinal as well as ritual ideas.

18. Next to the olive in importance comes the fig. The tree itself, with its dark broad green leaves above and light grey and glossy leaves beneath, its stem covered with a bark smooth and grey, and its boughs, that spread outwards with a pleasant shade, formed in conjunction with the vine one of the attractive features of an ancient Hebrew landscape, underneath whose shadows men loved to sit, so that the proverb of 'sitting under one's own vine and fig tree' became a current mode of expressing national prosperity (1 Kings iv. 25; Mic. iv. 4; Zech. iii. 10). In Jotham's parable (Judg. ix. 8 foll.) it comes second in the triumvirate of fruit trees—the olive, the fig, and the vine. Like the vine, it was made the subject of our Lord's parables. It was under a fig tree's

shade Nathanael sat (John i. 48) when Jesus first beheld him. The fig trees of Palestine grew by the wayside, and thus formed a welcome spectacle to the tired pilgrims (Matt. xxi. 18, 19) who sought relief from hunger as well as heat. This tree bore three kinds of fruit, viz. (1) The *early* fig (*bikkûrah*), which appeared about the end of June (after a mild winter), or in Jerusalem even earlier. From several passages in the prophets (Isa. xxviii. 4; Jer. xxiv. 2; Hos. ix. 10) we learn how highly this early fig was esteemed as a delicacy. They were not *gathered* from the tree, but, as in the case of the olive, the tree was shaken, and the ripe figs fell off 'into the mouth of the eater' (Nah. iii. 12). (2) The *summer figs*, which become ripe in August. Like the raisins, dried in masses from the grapes, these summer figs were dried into cakes and used as an article of consumption (called in Hebrew *debêlah*), especially by travellers (1 Sam. xxv. 18, xxx. 12). (3) The *winter figs* (or *phaggîm*), which remain hanging on the tree throughout the winter, after the tree has shed its leaves, and does not become ripe till the early part of the year, when the fresh leaves are ready to spring forth. These are longer than the summer figs, and have a dark violet colour (Winer).

The fig was also employed medicinally for boils and festers, and served as a poultice (2 Kings xx. 7), a use which was well known among the ancients.

It would lie beyond the purpose of this book to go into further detail respecting the fruits and cereals of Palestine. A brief enumeration must suffice.

The *date palm* flourished in Palestine (especially near Jericho) to a far greater extent than now. It marked the sacred spot where the prophetess Deborah exercised her gift (Judg. iv. 5),[1] and the Hebrew for 'palm' was used as a proper name for women (Tamar).

The *sycamore tree* was used for building material (Isa. ix. 10), and in ancient Egypt for furniture. Its fruit was eaten, but required special manipulation by puncturing a short time before it was gathered. This formed a distinct employment, as we learn from the prophet Amos (vii. 14). The tree was regarded as so valuable that a special overseer was appointed for its preservation (1 Chron. xxvii. 28).

The *pomegranate*, a bushy tree, not more than eight or ten feet high, with straight stem, reddish bark and lanceolate leaves, and round, red fruit, which ripens towards the end of August. The frequent mention of this tree in Scripture (Num. xiii. 23; Deut. viii. 8; 1 Sam. xiv. 2; Song of Songs iv 13, vii. 12; Joel i. 12; Hagg. ii. 19) sufficiently attests its importance.

Among cereals and other produce useful to man, *millet* (*dôchân*) is only mentioned once (in Ezek. iv. 9); *spelt*[2] (Exod. ix. 32; Isa. xxviii. 25), called *kussemeth* in Hebrew, was planted along the border of barley and wheat. Respecting other varieties mentioned in Isaiah xxviii. 25, we have not sufficiently certain means of identification. To these may be added *beans, lentils* and *cucumbers* (Isa. i. 8). *Garlic* (Num. xi. 5), *leeks, melons* and *onions* (*ibid.*) seem to have been Egyptian rather than Palestinian.

---

[1] On the original significance of the palm in ancient Semitic religion, see Robertson Smith's *Religion of the Semites*, p. 169.

[2] Unfortunately this is a matter of great doubt. The A.V. renders in Exodus ix. 32 by 'rye,' in Ezekiel iv. 9 by 'fitches.' The rendering of the R.V. is 'spelt,' and is supported by Delitzsch and Dillmann and most authorities (on Isa. xxviii. 25).

One growth of considerable importance we have left to the last, viz., that of *flax* (called *pésheth* or *pishtah*). It was planted very largely in the Egyptian delta, but was likewise a considerable product of Palestinian soil, as may be clearly seen from numerous notices in the Old Testament (Hos. ii. 5 ; Josh. ii. 6, etc.). On this subject the reader is referred to an earlier page (§ 8, p. 43).

19. We now come to **handicrafts**. Comparatively few of these were learned by the ancient Hebrews until the regal period, and it was to the Canaanites and Philistines, who occupied the coast lands, the Hebrews were chiefly indebted for whatever progress they made in the arts of life. Probably the frequent wars between Israel and surrounding races, and border raids carried on by either side, tended to check the progress of any civilizing influences, owing to the prevailing unsettlement. The wars with the Philistines must have had a very adverse influence. Of this we have a very significant illustration in 1 Samuel xiii. 19, where we read that during the wars of Saul 'there was no smith found throughout all the land of Israel, for the Philistines said, Lest the Hebrews make them swords or spears ; but all the Israelites went down to the Philistines, to sharpen every man his share, his hoe, his axe and his scythe (LXX.).

In the early nomadic stage of Israel's life the articles needed for daily use were simple and few. Even earthenware pots would be avoided as far as possible, because liable to break with the frequent migration of the clan. The preparation of skins for tent coverings or clothing, or the weaving of the wool for garments, would be the utmost stretch of handiwork to which the women of that primitive period would attain. The hides of slaughtered animals would also be required for the formation of the skin bottles so largely employed in Oriental antiquity to contain liquids (water, milk and wine), and also in making girdles, sandals and thongs (Benzinger). The earliest reference to the art of the *potter* is in 2 Samuel xvii. 28 (unless we take into account the 'pitchers' mentioned in the description of Gideon's night exploit, Judg. vii. 16), but it does not actually follow that the art was practised in Israel at that time. On the other hand, the references in the prophets (Isa. xxix. 16, and Jer. xviii. 2 foll., where the house of the potter is specially mentioned) show that during the regal period the art of shaping vessels from clay was learned by the Hebrews from their more highly civilized neighbours, and had become familiar. It is quite possible, indeed, that acquaintance with this and other handicrafts might have been acquired by early contact with the civilization of Egypt. There we know the art was practised from immemorial antiquity, and the soil furnished abundant material. According to Sir G. Wilkinson (*Manners and Customs of the Ancient Egyptians*, vol. iii. p. 163 foll.), the ancient Egyptian potters 'kneaded the clay with their feet, and after it had been properly worked up, they formed it into a mass of convenient size with the hand, and placed it on the wheel, which, to judge from that represented in the paintings, was of very simple construction, and turned with the hand. The various forms of the vases were made out by the finger during the revolution; the handles, if they had any, were afterwards affixed to them, and the devices and other ornamental parts were traced with a wooden or metal instrument previously to their being baked. They were then suffered to dry, and for this purpose were placed on planks of wood; they were afterwards arranged with great care on trays and carried, by means of the usual yoke borne on men's shoulders, to the oven.' This extract may sufficiently illustrate the process witnessed by the eyes of the prophet Jeremiah in the 'house of the potter' (Jer. xviii. 2). But it is extremely doubtful whether the Hebrews, even if they acquired this art in the land of the Pharaohs, could have preserved it during the long intervening period of desert wanderings, for desert life and the potter's art are hardly compatible things.

Recent researches in Palestine hardly lead us to Egypt as the proximate source of Hebrew skill in the potter's art. Israel must have learnt this, like their alphabet and so much else, from his Canaanite neighbours. And these neighbours were probably more influenced by Babylonian than by Egyptian civilization during the centuries that immediately preceded the age of Moses and Joshua. The inscriptions discovered at Tell el Amarna in Egypt (1887), combined with the yet more recent (1891) excavations conducted by Mr. Bliss in the old city of Lachish (now Tell el Ḥesî), have completely revolutionized our conceptions of the relations of Egypt and Western Asia in the 15th century B.C. Egypt was then a declining power. Between 1450 and 1400 (18th dynasty) Babylonian influence prevailed, as it had done long previously, in Syria and Palestine; and it had even reached Egypt itself. The discovery of more than 200 *cuneiform* tablets containing letters that passed between the Egyptian and Mesopotamian kings and between the former and their governors in Canaanite towns—all composed, *not* in hieroglyphic or cursive *Egyptian*, but in cuneiform *Babylonian*, touched with Canaanite words and forms of expression—clearly shows that we must begin to look elsewhere than to Egypt for the most potent moulding influences that ultimately shaped the civilization of ancient Israel, though we frequently detect the presence of another set of influences which were Egyptian (*e.g.* circumcision and alphabet). And surely this general result is confirmed by the notices of the earliest Hebrew historian, the Jehovist writer whose narrative begins with the section Genesis ii. 4–iv. 26, and is continued in considerable portions of chapters vi.–xi. As we read, our thoughts are continually directed to the Euphrates and Tigris, and not to the Nile.

The ancient Amorite (or Canaanite) pottery discovered at Tell el Hesî shows the early models of plastic art from which the ancient Hebrews borrowed. These early forms of pottery (1500–1000 B.C.) exhibit rough surfaces which present an appearance as though they had been combed over by a jagged stick. Many of the vessels exhibit stout bulging sides, as though they had been formed on the model of the yet earlier skins used for containing liquor.[1] Some of the

[1] In describing the Amorite pottery Flinders Petrie says, 'The combed face pottery is usually hand-made, though the brims are wheel-turned. It has been smoothed on the outside by scraping it down with a comb or notched edge of wood. The *ledge handles* are very striking, and quite unknown elsewhere. They belonged to large vessels with upright sides, and it is very possible that they were parts of the comb-face vessels. The thick-brim bowls are essentially Amorite, though the type lasted

forms of pottery (viz., clay pitchers) which Petrie, in his interesting work, *Tell el Hesy*, exhibits as specimens of ancient Jewish style, can only be described in the words of Benzinger as 'degenerate, coarse and

CLAY VESSEL FROM JERUSALEM.

inelegant' counterparts of the superior Phœnician workmanship. On the other hand, the specimens of pottery found in Jerusalem (figured in Perrot and

in a debased form into Jewish times, both in form and burnished facing. The earliest style of burnishing on the red face is with wide-open crossing lines, which yielded to closer patterns; and in late times a mere spiral burnishing made on the wheel. The red face is very bright in early cases, evidently a hæmatite colour in the Amorite times, though a dull ochre was used in Jewish imitations. . . . The forms are extravagant in some cases, but in general it is an excellent type for strength.'

Chipiez' *Histoire de l'Art*) show a far higher style of Hebrew art. Here the mouldings are more finished and graceful. In the clay vessels or jugs they run in parallel lines round the body or neck of the vessel. We see a strongly marked tendency to geometric figures in ornamentation, parallel and crossing lines, meandering lines as well as zigzags, squares, rhombi and triangles. Sometimes, in the larger Phœnician vases, we have different fields, separated by linear ornamentation, each field being filled with animal shapes, human figures and hunting scenes. We are reminded of the hunting scenes in Assyrian sculptures. But traces of Egyptian influence are not wanting. While we have the Babylonian palm, we also see the Egyptian lotus (Benzinger).

The process may be briefly described as follows: After the clay had been dug out and worked to a proper consistency by treading (Isa. xli. 25), it was placed on the potter's wheel, which consisted of one wooden disk revolving over another and larger. Both disks were called in Hebrew *obhnaim* (Jer. xviii. 3), and were worked by the feet. They revolved one over the other, and thus gave the curved shape and circular form to the vessels, just as in the case of a turning lathe. The existence of the potter's field near Jerusalem in the days of Isaiah (xxx. 14), comp. 1 Chron. iv. 23, shows that the industry had assumed considerable proportions towards the close of the 8th century B.C. The references to the potter's art in the Apocryphal literature indicate that it continued to occupy an important position. The Wisdom of Sirach xxxviii. 29, 30 contains a vivid description of the process. See also Wisdom of Solomon xv. 7.

20. **Weaving** was mainly the work of women. During the regal period even fabrics of an elaborate description were woven by them, as an interesting reference in 2 Kings xxiii. 7 clearly proves. This subject has been sufficiently treated in an earlier page (see § 8 on clothing, p. 42). Probably most of the finer textures were imported, as linen from Egypt, and silken damask from Damascus, in which the nobles of the time of Amos indulged (iii. 12 [1]), and which became famous throughout the East (called by the Arabs *dimaks*, and corrupted by the Greeks into *metaxa*). The looms of Babylonia were celebrated for their products, as the 'Shinar mantles' which excited Achan's cupidity (Josh. vii. 21) clearly testify. From the monumental representations of Assyria and Babylonia we can see that the kings and nobles were gorgeously arrayed. Specially rich was the embroidery.[2]

The Egyptian looms were of comparatively simple construction. They stood upright, and the shuttle was not thrown, but inserted with the hand. Among the Bedouin of the present day may be seen the most primitive form of weaving still existing. It might serve to represent the mode of operations pursued in the Hebrew household of early times. Among the Bedouin the cross threads are inserted by the fingers through the longitudinal threads, and the fabric is

---

[1] If we can trust either text or interpretation.
[2] See Tiele's *History of Babylonia and Assyria*, p. 602. The inscriptions of Assyrian monarchs from Asshur-nazir-pal to Asshurbanipal (9th to 7th century, B.C.) frequently mention embroidered linen garments among the spoil captured by them from the Western Asian nations that surrounded them, but the terms used to describe these garments have not yet been sufficiently fixed in their signification by Assyriologists.

then pressed close by the simple means of a piece of stick. It is impossible to tell how early the Hebrews learned the use of the shuttle. It is mentioned in the Book of Job (vii. 6), which cannot be placed earlier than the seventh century as a composition; but this furnishes us with no reliable basis of inference. It is to be noted, however, that Hebrew has no name for 'shuttle' as distinct from 'web.' The weaver's beam, to which the staff of Goliath's spear is compared (1 Sam. xvii. 7; comp. 2 Sam. xxi. 19), was a stout piece of wood belonging to the framework of the loom, running either horizontally or perpendicularly. Unfortunately, Judges xvi. 13, 14 is too obscure for us to employ it for purposes of illustration.

21. **Workmanship in wood, stone and metal** was not acquired in ancient Israel to any but moderate extent till the time of David and Solomon. At this time the Hebrews began to enter into relations with the greater civilized races of antiquity, viz., the Phœnicians and Aramæans. It is quite possible that, as in the case of weaving, so in the case of metal work, some of the traditions of Israel's long residence in Egypt may have been preserved. At any rate, the narrative of the making of the golden ephod at Gideon's shrine in Ophrah from the golden earrings, crescents and pendants captured from the Midianites, would suggest that the Hebrews understood, at least to some extent, the art of melting down the precious metals. It is not improbable, however, that Canaanites assisted in this operation. At this time *bronze* was the prevalent metal in use, rather than iron. Cooking utensils and fetters (Judg. xvi. 21) were made from it, and also armour, as helmet, shield, coat of

mail and greaves (1 Sam. xvii. 5, 6, referring to the arms of Goliath). Even spear and bow were made from the same metal (2 Sam. xxi. 16, xxii. 35). The material would be obtained from the copper mines of the Sinaitic peninsula. But it is quite as probable that it was also obtained from the Phœnicians, who owned the mines of Cyprus. In the time of David the tribute sent by Toi, King of Hamath, consisted of gold and silver vessels, and a considerable quantity of bronze, and these were dedicated by David to Jehovah (comp. the inscription of Tiglath Pileser I., col. iv. 1 foll.). The use of *iron* was chiefly confined to the head or point of arms or implements (as the spear, ploughshare, or axe). Among the Canaanites chariots were plated with iron (Judg. i. 19). Probably its use did not become prevalent till two centuries after the time of Solomon. Thus, in the triumphal inscriptions from Kalah, in Assyria, of Ramman-nirâri III., we read (in line 19) that he captured from the King of Syria, whom he completely overthrew, 5,000 talents of iron, together with 3,000 of copper and 2,300 of silver. But this did not occur till nearly two centuries after the time of David. On the other hand, Tiglath Pileser I., an Assyrian conqueror who lived just a century before David (*i.e.* about 1100 B.C.), frequently mentions bronze or copper, but never iron, among the objects of plunder or tribute. We find also that Asshurnazir-pal and Shalmanezer II., Assyrian kings who reigned about a century after David, only refer occasionally to iron. Bronze or copper is chiefly mentioned, together with gold, silver and lead. These results coincide with the data of the Old Testament.

Certainly the general impressions left by the narratives in the Books of Judges and 1 Samuel, together with the striking evidence afforded by 1 Samuel xiii. 19, 20 (referred to on a previous page), would not dispose us to build too much upon Egyptian influence. The turning-point in the history of Hebrew handicrafts was the introduction of Phœnician workmen into Israel's Southern capital in the reign of David (2 Sam. v. 11).

The ordinary name for a worker in wood or metal, or even stone, is *chârâsh*. Of this a good illustration is afforded by 2 Samuel v. 11, where the same word is used in the plural in both cases—'workers of wood and workers of wall stone.' The same prefix would be used for a worker in metals, the word for the metal defining the art. The word *chârâsh* in Hebrew signifies properly to cut or grave any surface, and hence is used for ploughing the soil. It is this word which is used to express all the operations of mechanical skill, as that of a smith or carpenter. For cleaving open or *hewing* wood and stone another term is employed (*chatzab*). But it must be remembered that these are also Canaanite words. An immense impulse to the exercise of these different manual crafts was doubtless communicated by the residence of Hiram's workmen in Jerusalem. The very fact that Solomon should have found it necessary to hire Sidonian wood cutters (1 Kings v. 6; Heb. xx.), because 'there is not any among us that knows how to fell timber like the Sidonians,' is ample proof that the Hebrews even in that day were but indifferent workmen. We are not therefore surprised to learn that all the skilled work of the new temple, as the fine mouldings in bronze and the richly ornamented capitals of the columns, with representations of pomegranate and the 'brazen sea,' of which so elaborate a description is given in 1 Kings vii. 13-51, was the product of the skill of a celebrated Tyrian artificer whose services Solomon was fortunate enough to obtain.

At the time of which we are now speaking (about 975 B.C.) the life of Israel was almost entirely agricultural where it was not pastoral. This is clearly apparent from 1 Kings v. 11, in which we are told that Solomon paid Hiram in corn and oil a regulated quantity annually for the services rendered by the Phœnician skilled artizans. And it is probable that these relations between the two peoples remained for some time on this footing, agricultural produce being given in exchange for the products of Phœnician skill. The story of the iron axe head (used for hewing out beams) which fell from the prophet's hand into the water (2 Kings vi. 5) gives us a useful hint of the growth of handicrafts among the ancient Hebrews. We may presume, however, that the axe head itself was not forged in Hebrew furnaces, but was either imported or was the product of the skill of resident Phœnician workmen, whom the policy of Ahab and Jezebel had introduced into Israel. The dynasty of Omri brought Israel and Phœnicia into such intimate relations that the influence on Hebrew culture must have been permanently felt in Judah as well as Ephraim.

Moreover, as foreign, and especially Canaanite and Philistine population, came to be absorbed into the Hebrew nation, their skill found a domicile among the cities of Israel. The close relations which subsisted between the Philistines and David in the time of Saul brought them in considerable numbers (especially from Gath) into the towns of Israel, and their superior skill in weaving and forging (Judg. xvi. 11-14; 1 Sam. xiii. 19) doubtless made itself felt. In the reign of Jehoash, about 120 years after Solomon's temple was built, when repairs became necessary, we have no hint of foreign workmen being required among the stone masons, carpenters and builders hired for the purpose (2 Kings xii. 7-13). The mention of the plumb line by Amos (vii. 7 foll.), and also his references to luxurious dwelling houses (iii. 15, etc.), combine to show that the art of building was familiar to his countrymen in the middle of the 8th century B.C. Moreover, it had long been the custom for water cisterns to be hollowed out of the limestone rock for the use of herds, as well as for orchards, vineyards and pleasure gardens. In the reign of Hezekiah a work of considerable public utility was carried out in the construction of a pool and conduit for the purpose of bringing water into the city (2 Kings xx. 20). This is to be identified with the conduit which brought the water of the Virgin's Spring by a subterranean passage into the Pool of Siloam.

A recent discovery, fully described by Prof. Sayce (*Fresh Light from the Ancient Monuments*, pp. 98-106), has revealed an important inscription concealed at the bottom of the pool, which describes how this considerable engineering feat was carried out. The inscription records the interesting fact that the excavation, which is about 600 yards in length, was begun at both ends. Observation confirms this statement, as the marks of the pickaxes or other boring instruments run in opposite directions in the southern, as compared with the northern, half of the tunnel. In the 4th line of the inscription we read that the hewers at last hewed against one another, axe against axe, and the waters flowed from the channel into the pool. The curves and other irregularities in the tunnel show that various ineffectual attempts were made to meet, until at length they were crowned with success.

Reference has already been made to the ever-growing civilization and luxury of Israel and Judah from the 10th century to the 7th, to which the prophetic writings of the last two centuries frequently bear witness. The more luxurious dwellings presuppose the presence of the skilled workmen. Smelting and forging thus became familiar arts, and the extraction of iron and copper ore from the mountains (Deut. viii. 9) was a process which the Hebrews in the course of centuries had acquired. Smelting of ore and the refinement of gold and silver from dross are metaphors which constantly occur in the Psalms as expressive of spiritual testing (Ps. xii. 6; xvii. 3, xxvi. 2, cv. 19; comp. Isa. i. 22, 25). It is a fact worth noting that, when at length Jerusalem was captured by the Babylonian invader, as many as 1,000 locksmiths and other skilled mechanics were deported from the city (2 Kings xxiv. 16).

Goldsmiths and silversmiths made use of alkali in the purification of the metal (Isa. i. 25). From Isaiah xl. 19, xli. 7 we learn that one very important branch of their industry consisted in the manufacture of idols. Upon a basis of wood that is well seasoned and free from decay the gold is overlaid by the goldsmith in plates. To the gold plates are soldered silver chains, with the object of fastening the image to its niche. The gold plates are previously prepared by beating them out upon an anvil, after which they are fixed upon the image by means of nails. It is a significant circumstance that the words for 'anvil,' 'hammer,'[1] 'nail,' 'bellows,' 'furnace,' and 'crucible,' belong almost entirely to the literature of the 7th and following centuries. 'Axe' and 'saw,' instruments for working wood, are mentioned by Isaiah (x. 15), who belonged to the 8th century. The same writer shows familiarity with the ideas of hewing stone and building. He also uses the word *chéret*, meaning both *stilus* and 'chisel.' Isaiah i. 22, 25 presupposes a considerable acquaintance with the art of refining the precious metals.

22. **Writing** must have been practised in ancient Israel from the days of Moses downwards. Not only does Scripture itself furnish evidence for this, but it is also established by a very large array of archæological evidence. The statements of the Old Testament are very explicit that the Ten Commandments were inscribed on two stone tables (Exod. xxiv. 12, xxxi. 18, xxxii. 15 foll.); also that Moses recorded the stages of the journeys of the children of Israel in the wilderness (Num. xxxiii. 2), and that he commanded

[1] One word for 'hammer' (*makkabah*) is found, not only in Isaiah xliv. 6, but also in 1 Kings vi. 7, and in nearly the same form in Judges iv. 21; but it is worth notice that in the ancient song of Deborah (Judg. v. 26) another word is employed, meaning a 'beater' or mallet (made of wood). The *makkabah* meant something made of hard metal for beating, breaking through, or *hollowing* out, as the etymology shows. The same root occurs in the inscription that describes the *boring* of the tunnel to the pool of Siloam.

the Hebrews (Deut. xxvii. 2-4) that after crossing over Jordan, large stones, plastered with plaster, should be inscribed with the words of the law (comp. Josh. viii. 32).

The age of Moses is comparatively modern in the great time chart of human history revealed to us by archæology, and it has long been a well-ascertained fact that the art of writing had been understood and practised in the valleys of the Nile and of the Euphrates for about 3,000 years before the Exodus. Respecting the complicated cuneiform or wedge-shaped signs employed in Babylonia, the reader is referred to the interesting chapter by Dr. Budge, of the British Museum, in his work *Babylonian Life and History* (p. 100 foll.). In Egypt the system of writing was that which is called hieroglyphic, or, in abbreviated form, hieratic. Now it might naturally be expected that the latter form of writing would be that which the Hebrew leader of the Exodus would have employed. About this it is impossible to form any satisfactory conclusion. The use of the Babylonian cuneiform system by the princes of Egypt and by the Egyptian prefects of the Canaanite towns about 1400 B.C. is a fact which has been recently brought to light by the discovery of cuneiform-written clay tablets at Tell el Amarna. More recently still a similar tablet, inscribed with cuneiform, belonging to the same period, has been discovered at Tell el Ḥesî, the site of the ancient Lachish. These facts simply prove that cuneiform writing was known and practised in Canaan in the age which immediately preceded that of Moses; but it would be extremely rash with our present knowledge to draw any inference except this: that it is possible that Moses understood and employed the Babylonian cuneiform as well as language in his legislative documents. But such a supposition is hardly probable, unless we have the right to assume that a considerable number of Israelites could read and understand Babylonian cuneiform. But who could have the hardihood to assert this of a race of nomads? It is more within the bounds of probability that a simpler system of writing of an alphabetic nature was commonly employed by the Hebrews and Canaanites of that period, out of which the Phœnician alphabet sprang, which has become the parent of all the alphabets of the world. It is quite true that we have no specimen of this writing earlier than the inscription on the Moabite Stone belonging to the 9th century B.C. But such a simple and well-wrought system of representing speech—so far superior to the clumsy and complicated phonetic signs of Babylonia—obviously did not come into existence suddenly. Further researches will probably show that it was gradually elaborated in the course of centuries from a more complex ideographic and syllabic system of writing. It was this simpler alphabetic system in its earlier stage that Moses, Joshua, and their followers probably employed.

The material upon which the characters were inscribed was, in the first instance, stone. They were written with a graving tool or chisel, which in later days came to approximate a *stilus* in shape. This appears to have been the common form of pen used in the days of Isaiah, and which he calls the *stilus* or pen (*chéret*) 'of a man' (*i.e.* ordinary pen). In the time of Jeremiah it was called an *'ēt*, and made of iron. The polished tablet upon which Isaiah wrote was either of stone or wood (Isa. viii. 1). That wood was occasionally the material selected, seems to be indicated by Numbers xvii. 2, Ezekiel xxxvii. 16. Tablets of clay, marked when moist, and then dried and baked, may also have been used, if we can allow Ezekiel iv. 1 to be quoted as an authority. Ezekiel, however, was probably largely influenced by his Babylonian surroundings, where clay tablets were universally employed. Therefore, the 'tile' on which Jerusalem was portrayed can hardly be quoted as a precedent for ordinary Hebrew and Palestinian usage. On the other hand, the early employment of clay tablets in Palestine by the Egyptian governors, to which the Tell el Amarna documents bear witness, lends some plausibility to the supposition that they may have been used by ancient Israel. The most common material for documents was probably *dressed skins*, or in some cases *papyrus*. The fact that these documents assumed the form of a *roll* (*megillah*), wound round a staff, clearly shows that they must have consisted of some pliant material like those just mentioned. The Septuagint rendering of Jeremiah xxxvi. 2 indicates that the roll book there mentioned consisted of Egyptian papyrus or parchment, the *charta* used by the Greeks and Romans, of which Pliny enumerates as many as eight different qualities. When we bear in mind the close relations that subsisted between Egypt and Palestine in the 7th century, the hint afforded by this rendering of the Greek translators is very probable. The 'ink' mentioned in the same chapter (verse 18) was either red or black. Obviously the kind of pen that was used was not the iron stilus. This could only be employed by scratching the surface of wood, or stone, or dried leaves of the palm, as is done in South India at the present day. For writing with ink on papyrus the Hebrews, in the time of Jeremiah, made use of a reed pen. The point of this was sharpened by means of a special 'secretary's knife,' also used for cutting paper (Jer. xxxvi. 23). It was, no doubt, almost exactly the same in form as the *arundo* or reed pen, used for writing on paper by the ancient Romans, of which a representation taken from a Pompeian painting is given in Rich's *Dictionary of Roman and Greek Antiquities* (with an *atramentarium*, or inkstand, close beside it). This again, like the paper or papyrus, was borrowed from ancient Egypt. The ink vessel may, perhaps, have been of the nature of a *palette*, as in ancient Egypt.[1] In any case it was carried about the person, suspended by the loins, as we learn from Ezekiel ix. 2, 3, 11.

The political importance of the art of writing among the great civilized races of antiquity is clearly indicated by Prof. Ed. Meyer in his *History of Egypt*.[2] It creates a great gulf between the educated class and the masses, the former consisting of the young officials connected with the court and those who were trained by the priesthood of the temples. It would be difficult to say how far this was true of Israel during the regal period. It must be remembered that the Canaanite system of writing was *alphabetic*, and much simpler. It was therefore far

---

[1] Meyer's *History of Egypt* (in German), p. 54. Excellent illustrations may be found in this work, pp. 55, 56, 161.
[2] *Ibid.*, p. 55.

more easy of acquisition than the difficult and complex systems of Babylonia and Egypt, which would need considerable time and labour to learn to apply successfully. In the 8th century writing was very largely practised in Israel, as the oracles of the prophets frequently testify (Hos. viii. 12). Isaiah deplores the large number of unrighteous enactments that were recorded (Isa. x. 1). Yet there must have remained a considerable uneducated class who were unable to read, as the same prophet affirms in another passage (xxix. 12), and their ignorance of writing not only acted as a social barrier, but in the presence of so much gross injustice and social oppression must have aggravated their poverty.

We know that there arose in connection with the court from the time of David and Solomon a special class of officials called *scribes*. It would form a part of their duties to write out the court or royal annals. Thus in the time of David we already find the *recorder* and the *scribe*, or secretary of state, among the regularly appointed court officials (2 Sam. viii. 17, xx. 25; comp. 2 Kings xviii. 18, etc.). It has been supposed by most writers that the 'recorder's' function was that of court or imperial annalist, and this seems on the whole more probable than the view of Nowack, who would apparently restrict his duties to that of being simply king's remembrancer. The 'scribe' or secretary's duty would include that of being the king's *amanuensis*. He would accompany the monarch, whether at home or on military expeditions. The Persian monarchs had several such officers in continuous attendance. As we learn from Herodotus (viii. 90, *ad fin.*), they formed a part of the staff of King Xerxes when he was watching the battle of Salamis. The fatal despatch concerning Uriah which David sent to Joab (2 Sam. xi. 14) was in all probability penned by his secretary, Seraiah (chap. viii. 17). Whether that clever and unscrupulous Phœnician, Jezebel, needed the services of a secretary in her nefarious plot (1 Kings xxi. 8) might perhaps be doubted. But as we learn that she employed the royal seal, and it may reasonably be held that this was kept by the royal secretary, it is probable that his services were employed in writing the despatch to the elders that was to compass Naboth's doom.

23. The constant use of writing in business transactions, as contracts of sale and purchase, leads us to speak of **seals**. Of them we have frequent mention in the Old Testament. They were usually worn as rings either on the finger or hung by a cord round the neck. How ancient the latter usage was we may infer from Genesis xxxviii. 18, while the antiquity of the habit of wearing signet rings on the finger is indicated by the honour conferred upon Joseph by Pharaoh in Genesis xli. 42. At the present day the custom in Egypt is to wear it on the little finger of the right hand (Delitzsch). But it is to Babylonia rather than to Egypt that we must look for the custom of using seals in the attestation of documents. There the tradition goes back to a hoary antiquity. Babylonia is the land of contract tablets. Dr. Budge, of the British Museum, says: 'We have many thousands in our national collection, as many as 5,000 were unpacked at one time. They record loans of money and produce, the sale of houses, fields, and wheat, marriage deeds and dowries, sales of

slaves, notices of loans paid, promissory notes,' etc. 'At times the contract tablet has been placed in a clay envelope, and upon the outside a copy of the contract within has been inscribed. On the one side (obverse) the contract and contracting parties' names are stated, on the other (reverse) comes the list of witnesses, and at the bottom follows the date, the name of the king, and his country. Often these tablets bear impressions of the seals of the witnesses; the poor man impressed the mark of his nail.' Numerous examples of such deeds of sale are to be found in Dr. Budge's *Babylonian Life and History*, p. 113 foll.

Fortunately we possess several specimens of ancient Palestinian seals and seal rings, which clearly show that even among the Hebrews the art of carving and engraving stone was probably acquired from the Phœnicians at an early date. Most of the seal rings are merely oval stones. Frequently the ring simply contained the name of the owner engraved upon it. One very interesting specimen must have belonged to an ancient Hebrew, and, to judge from the antiquity of the characters, it came from a comparatively early time. It bears the legend in Hebrew, 'Belonging to Obadiah, servant of the king.' Other interesting examples may be found figured in Dr. Benzinger's valuable work on Hebrew Archæology (p. 258 foll.). One excellent representation of a seal ring comes from Cyprus. Other seals exhibit ornamentations of various kinds. On one we have the Phœnician palm leaf. On another what looks like a wreath of pomegranate or poppy. We have also Hebrew seals with legends stating that they belong 'to Shemaiah, the son of Azariah,' 'to

Nethaniah, the son of Obadiah,' 'to Hananiah, the son of Achbor,' 'to Hananiah, the son of Azariah,' and 'to Shebaniah, servant of Uzziah.' One seal is of particular interest because the inscription clearly proves it to have been Moabite. It belonged 'to Chemosh-yechi,' a proper name which signifies 'May Chemosh live' (comp. Amos viii. 14).

The details of the preceding pages will enable the reader to realize more vividly the descriptions of the purchase for seventeen shekels of the field in Anathoth by the prophet Jeremiah (Jer. xxxii. 6–15). Witnesses were appended to the deed of purchase, just as in the case of the Babylonian contracts just described, and it was sealed with Jeremiah's own seal (verse 10).

24. In **trade** with other nations it cannot be said that the Hebrews before the exile played any very prominent part. The Phœnicians in those days did most of the carrying trade of the world. They in fact occupied in the ancient world the same place that the English do in the modern. The comparative simplicity of their language and writing made it admirably suited for the needs of a mercantile race. On the other hand, the Hebrews always shrank from the sea. The pictures of the ocean in Hebrew literature are never pleasing (Ps. cvii. 23–30). The wicked are compared to it (Isa. lvii. 20; Jude 13), and it is banished from the paradise of the Apocalypse (Rev. xxi. 1). The potent cause for this was the configuration of Palestine, and the nature of the coast, rocky and precipitous, from Akko to Carmel, which affords the only considerable bay along this Canaanite border. South of Carmel the flat alluvial

land contains scarcely a single stream of any importance. The smallness of the estuaries and the absence of bays combine to render this part of the coast almost useless for navigation. For these geographical reasons, as Nowack has recently shown, the Hebrews were excluded from life on the sea. Doubtless other causes, as the presence of the Philistines along the coast, and Israel's nomadic and agricultural occupations, co-operated to debar them from that career of naval traders (*mercatores*) to which the Ionians and Phœnicians (pre-eminently the latter) devoted themselves. Solomon, as we know from 1 Kings ix. 26 foll., x. 11 foll., 22, availed himself of the naval supremacy of the Phœnicians to establish by means of their vessels and sailors mercantile voyages to Ophir (probably on the western coast of India) from Ezion-geber, near Elath, on the Red Sea. These Phœnician vessels brought into Palestine gold and silver, precious stones, ivory, sandal wood, apes and peacocks. These trading voyages occupied three years (1 Kings x. 22), and as the freight carried by the vessels was considerable, it was necessary that they should be of superior size. The name given to vessels of this character was 'ships of Tarshish.' Tarshish was the Hebrew name of Tartessus in Spain, one of the Phœnician trade settlements, from which, as Ezekiel tells us (Ezek. xxvii. 12, 24), silver, iron, tin and lead were exported to Tyre. Since the vessels sent to Tarshish were of larger construction, all those of similar build were called 'Tarshish ships,' just as we in modern times speak of 'Indiamen' (Isa. ii. 16; Ps. xlviii. 7).

Unfortunately for Israel, this valuable outlet and

inlet for commerce through Ezion-geber could only be held under control by also holding Edom as a vassal province. But between Edom and Israel there existed the long-standing feud symbolized in the patriarchal narratives of Esau and Jacob.

This fact tended to impair the value of this southern naval port. In the days of Jehoshaphat an attempt was made to restore the naval prosperity of Ezion-geber, this time without the aid of Phœnician mariners, but the inexpert Hebrews met with utter disaster, and, despite the solicitations of Ahaziah, the attempt was not renewed (1 Kings xxii. 48 foll.). Palestine is the natural highway of communication for the caravan companies that from the earliest times have carried the merchandise of the Northern and North-western races of Western Asia (Assyria, Syria and Phœnicia, the Hittites) to Egypt, and *vice versâ* (Gen. xxxvii. 28). Yet the track which they followed passed through the coast land of the Philistines rather than through Central Canaan, which was occupied by the Hebrews. Those traders who passed through Israelite territory were obliged to pay a certain toll (1 Kings x. 15). Nearly all were Phœnicians, hence the name in Hebrew for 'merchant' is Canaanite (or Phœnician). But gradually after the time of Solomon the Hebrews themselves became traders, and in the Northern kingdom during the 8th century B.C. acquired considerable wealth in the pursuit. But the name 'Canaanite' was still employed in the general sense of trader (Isa. xxiii. 8; Job xli. 6; Prov. xxxi. 24). It is in this sense Hosea, describing Ephraim (xii. 7, 8 foll.), says, 'As for Canaan, the balances of deceit are in his hand, he loves to defraud. And

Ephraim thought: Nevertheless I have become rich, I have gotten myself property.' Here the word 'Canaan' stands for the entire mercantile class with which Ephraim had become identified.

For purposes of trade the Hebrews not infrequently emigrated to foreign cities, and occupied entire streets or special quarters with their bazaars. Thus in the time of Ahab a special treaty was concluded with the Syrian king, which enacted that such special quarters should be provided in Damascus for the Hebrews, and in Samaria for the Syrians. During the Assyrian wars against Palestine of the 8th and 7th centuries, doubtless a large number of Hebrew traders settled in Egypt and other foreign countries, and originated in this way that great dispersion of the race which has ever since become a permanent factor in the history of the people and of the world. We know that in Babylonia there existed a great business firm in the days of Nebuchadnezzar, owned by an individual or family called Egibi, of which an immense number of contract tablets have been preserved. As Egibi appears to be the exact Babylonian equivalent of the Hebrew Jacob, it is not improbable that we may here see a great Oriental forerunner of the modern Rothschilds. During the exile the policy recommended by Jeremiah xxix. 5–7 was faithfully carried out, and the exiled Jews, many among whom were skilled mechanics (2 Kings xxiv. 16), settled down peacefully and became successful tradesmen (Ezek. iii. 24, xxxiii. 30, shows that they possessed houses of their own).

25. **Etiquette** and **social intercourse**. Orientals have ever been punctilious in their use of

forms. Even an equal is always addressed 'My lord,' while the speaker talks of himself as 'Thy servant' (slave), or, if a woman, 'Thy handmaid' (*lit.* slave girl, 1 Sam. i. 18). When the person addressed is in a superior social or official position, the speaker becomes still more deferential and ceremonious, and expresses this feeling by putting the word for 'lord' in the plural number, which gives it the force of an abstract, and thus conveys greater dignity (just as we speak of 'your highness'). Even Elijah speaks of Ahab under this conventional form of respect due to a king (1 Kings xviii. 11). But this falls far short of the terms of obsequious and even grovelling homage with which Oriental monarchs in ancient times were usually treated. Specimens of the epistolary style in which the kings of Egypt were addressed by the Canaanite governors (15th century B.C.) have been preserved for us in some of the despatches of the Tell el Amarna collections of tablets. Thus in the series of letters from Abimelech, Governor of Tyre, to the Egyptian Pharaoh, contained in Dr. Bezold's *Oriental Diplomacy*, the formal opening of each dispatch reads as follows: 'To the king, my lord, my god,[1] my sun. Thus doth Abimelech, thy servant, prostrate himself seven times, and yet seven times under the feet of the king my lord. I am dust beneath the shoe of the king my lord,' etc.

The above extract refers to the custom of prostration before the presence of a superior. Even before one who was not far different in rank a Hebrew

---

[1] Literally 'gods,' a plural expressive of dignity, just as in the case of the Hebrew name for 'God,' and also that for 'Lord.'

would bow down with his face to the earth three or even seven times, in token of respect, as David before Jonathan (1 Sam. xx. 41), and Jacob before his brother Esau (Gen. xxxiii. 3). Whenever the superior was met by an inferior who was riding at the time on an ass, mule, or camel, the latter would dismount and perform the customary act of obeisance by bowing with the face to the earth. A woman like Abigail, even though she was the wife of a wealthy shaich, showed this act of deference in the presence of a powerful chief like David (1 Sam. xxv. 23). The betrothed Rebekah showed like courtesy to her destined husband Isaac (Gen. xxiv. 64). It was a universal custom for men who were on friendly terms to kiss each other, both on meeting (Gen. xxxiii. 4), and also on departure (Acts xx. 37. In Ruth i. 14 the reference is to women). Kissing was not always on the mouth. From 2 Samuel xx. 9 we may infer that kissing on the beard was the ordinary form of salutation when the acquaintance was not intimate. In modern Egypt, according to Lane, it is customary for a man 'to kiss the hand of a superior . . . and then to put it to his forehead, in order to pay him particular respect; but in most cases the latter does not allow this, and only touches the hand that is extended toward his; the other person then merely puts his own hand to his lips and forehead . . . The slaves and servants of a grandee kiss their lord's sleeve or the skirt of his clothing.' Submission to potentates was expressed by kissing the feet. The inscriptions of Tiglath Pileser III. and other Assyrian monarchs constantly mention the performance of this mode of homage by conquered kings ('they kissed my feet'). Probably this is the act of submission referred to by the Psalmist in the phrase, 'Kiss the Son, lest He be angry' (Ps. ii. 12), and it is quite in accordance with modern usage, for 'to testify abject submission in craving pardon for an offence or interceding for another person, or begging any favour of a superior, not infrequently the feet are kissed instead of the hand' (Lane). The kissing of the Pope's toe is nothing but an old Oriental usage lingering in modern Christendom. The words with which the ancient Israelites saluted one another are nearly identical with those used by a modern Arab, viz., 'Peace (or well-being) unto you' (Judg. xix. 20). Or sometimes it was thrown into the form of a question. 'Is it peace unto you?' (= How are you?), after which similar inquiries are made after the welfare of near kindred, as husband, father, brothers, or children. Oriental etiquette, however, avoided mention of the wife (2 Kings iv. 26; Gen. xliii. 27; 2 Sam. xi. 7). Occasionally the phrase was varied by using the expression which was addressed by Boaz to his reapers, 'Jehovah be with you,' to which they reply, 'May Jehovah bless you' (Ruth ii. 4). In bidding farewell the ancient Hebrew said, 'Go in peace' (1 Sam. i. 17; 2 Sam. xv. 9; Luke viii. 48; John xiv. 27). Visits to one another by persons in high social position were accompanied by gifts, sometimes called by the Hebrews 'blessing' (since the word to bless in Hebrew means to greet, or to bid farewell to a person). Instances of this usage may be found in Genesis xxxiii. 11; 1 Samuel xxv. 27, xxx. 26; 2 Kings v. 5, viii. 9. In response to these gifts others were bestowed in return (1 Kings x. 10, 13).

Respect for elders was the universal rule of ancient Semitic society. Among the Arab nomads of the present day it is the elders or shaichs who wield most authority in the clan, and much the same position was held by the Hebrew 'elders.' Even in ancient Egypt the rule of politeness prevailed: 'Sit not when an elder stands,' and a similar tradition of courtesy on the part of the younger towards the elder finds expression in the Old Testament (Job xxix. 8; Lev. xix. 32).

Buying and *Selling* involves a tedious process of bargaining, until some price at last is reached somewhere midway between demand on the part of the seller, and offer on that of the buyer. At the outset it is not uncommon for the seller to say to the buyer, when the latter enquires the price, 'Receive it as a present' (implying that the cost is such a trifle). The seller knows, however, that advantage will not be taken of what is universally accepted as a mere form of speech. It is in this sense (as Delitzsch has shown) we must take Ephron the Hittite's offer of the field and cave of Machpelah as a gift to Abraham (Gen. xxiii. 11). The following verses show that a price is settled without further demur.

This interesting transaction took place at the *gate of the city*, the universal place of concourse, where public and private affairs were discussed (Prov. xxxi. 23, 31; Ps. lxix. 12), where suits between individuals were decided and wrongs redressed (2 Sam. xv. 2 foll., xix. 8 foll.; Job xxix. 7 foll.). It was at this place the elders of the city assembled and witnessed the formal act of taking off the shoe, whereby Boaz testified his purchase of the property of Elimelech and his sons from the hand of Naomi, and that he had purchased Ruth as his wife (Ruth iv. 8, 9).

Hospitality in ancient times was an all-prevailing rule of life, and mitigated the stern conditions of primitive Oriental society, which regarded every member of an alien clan as a natural enemy. But if as a sojourner and alien he sought the protection of any member of the clan he visited, this was freely afforded. The partaking of the common meal constituted a temporary bond of brotherhood. The head of the house regarded his visitor as one of his own household during the period of the sojourner's stay, and resented any injury done to him as a personal affront. Illustrations may be found in numerous passages of the Old Testament: Genesis xviii., xix.; Judges xix. 15, 20 foll.; Job xxxi. 32. The existing traditions of modern Syria and Arabia in respect of hospitality, described by Burckhardt, Robinson, Shaw, and other travellers, are merely a continuance of this ancient custom. The slaves of the household fetched water to wash the feet of the visitors (Gen. xviii. 4; Luke vii. 44), while the hair of the head was anointed with some fragrant unguent (Amos vi. 6; Psalm xxiii. 5; Luke vii. 46). The fatted calf or kid is slain, and the best of the meal is kneaded to make cakes. The master of the household does not join in the repast, but stands and waits upon his guests (Gen. xviii. 8).

There were only *two actual meals* in the day in the life of an Oriental. The first was about mid-day (Gen. xliii. 16; 1 Kings xx. 16; Ruth ii. 14), corresponding to the Greek *ariston* (Luke xi. 37, xiv. 12); the second, which was the chief meal of the day, corresponded to the Greek *deipnon*, and took place in the evening (Judg. xix. 21). The Passover was also celebrated at this time (Exod. xvi. 12).

In primitive times probably a mat served the place of a table, just as we find among the Arabs at the present day. Those who partook sat cross-legged upon mats or other coverings spread upon the ground. Numerous references show that women also participated (1 Sam. i. 8; Deut. xvi. 11; Ruth ii. 14, etc.). With the growth of civilization the use of tables was introduced. In Amos vi. 4 we read of the wealthy nobles reclining at their banquets upon elaborate divans. This presupposes the use of a table, the existence of which in superior Hebrew dwellings is clearly shown by 2 Kings iv. 10; Ezek. xxiii. 41, and other indications. The divan held from three to five persons. One would recline with feet outstretched behind him, resting upon his left arm, while the right was free to reach the viands on the table. His neighbour rested with the hinder part of his head touching the breast of the former (Nowack). This was the attitude of the beloved desciple (John xiii. 23). The meat was eaten with the fingers. It came to the table cut in small pieces, and was taken out of the dish. We also read in Judges vi. 19 foll., Isaiah lxv. 4, of thick broth made from flesh and other materials. Cakes and bread were dipped in this broth and eaten (comp. Ruth ii. 14; Matt. xxvi. 23). After the meal was over the hands were washed in water.

Respecting the use of wine in banquets we have already spoken in § 16. Numerous references in the oracles of the prophets show that the feasting was enlivened by music. Isaiah, in a graphic passage

(Isa. v. 12), mentions the lute, cymbal, tambourine, and flute.

26. **Death** and **Funeral Customs.** The Hebrews, like the other ancient Semites, held to a belief in the continuance of life after death in the shadowy underworld called *Sheôl*. Not only necromancy or the conjuration of the spirits of the dead (1 Sam. xxviii. 7-19), against which prophecy and law protested alike (Isa. viii. 19; Deut. xviii. 11), but also the ordinary phrases and customs of a pious Hebrew of ancient times, are obviously based upon this belief, that the spirits of the dead are still existent and potent. Thus the continuance of the life of the ancestors of one's family in a family life in the underworld impelled a Hebrew to preserve with care the burial ground containing the sepulchres of his fathers, and to desire above all things 'to be gathered to his fathers' in shadowy Hades.

After death the eyes were closed. To a parent this duty would ordinarily be performed by the eldest son (comp. Gen. xlvi. 4). In the New Testament we read that the body was washed (Acts ix. 37), anointed with perfumed oil (Mark xvi. 1), and wrapped in cloths (Matt. xxvii. 59). But this appears to have been later practice, and coincides with the Greek custom in the matter of washing and anointing. The embalming of the body in the case of Jacob and Joseph (Gen. l. 2, 26) was merely the application of an Egyptian usage foreign to Israel. Whether it was the custom of the Hebrews to bury a man in his characteristic or professional attire, *e.g.* a king with his crown, a warrior with his sword and spear, etc., is by no means clear. The apparition of Samuel (1 Sam.

xxviii. 14) in his prophetic mantle only suggests this, but considerable support is given to it in Ezekiel xxxii. 27, which seems to indicate that it was customary to bury a soldier with his weapons.

There is no definite proof in the Old Testament that the bodies were ever burned (Amos vi. 10, 1 Sam. xxxi. 12, are too uncertain to quote). They were usually buried in rocky hollows. Occasionally, as in the case of Petra, the sepulchres were hollowed out of a rocky cliff at an almost inaccessible height, and were adorned with elaborate portal and frieze. This, however, was a much later embellishment. Frequently the rock was hollowed out into a large chamber, and in some cases into galleries. The corpses were then placed horizontally in hollows made in the sides of the wall, about six feet long and about eighteen inches in breadth and height. Or the body might simply be deposited upon a stone ledge cut out of rock about two feet high and with an arch above it. Or in some cases troughs were cut in the wall of rock.

The body was carried to the grave upon a bier, called *mittah*, the ordinary Hebrew word for bed (2 Sam. iii. 31; Gen. xlvii. 31). Mourners followed, who made the air resound with their lamentations. Sometimes mourning women were hired for this special purpose, who beat their breasts and uttered loud shrieks, like the women to whom Ezekiel refers (viii. 14) as mourning for Tammuz. The exclamations generally took the form, 'Ah, my brother!' or 'Ah, sister!' or 'Ah, lord!' 'Ah, his glory!' (Jer. xxii. 18; 1 Kings xiii. 30), uttered in a regular rhythmic form. Sometimes poems or dirges were composed

K

and recited for the occasion, and it is interesting to note that among the earliest fragments of literature in the Old Testament we have two dirges composed by King David—one the lament over Saul and Jonathan, entitled the 'bow,' which a choir was trained to recite (2 Sam. i. 17-27), and another briefer elegy over Abner (2 Sam. iii. 33, 34). From Jeremiah xlviii. 36 we infer that players on flutes accompanied the dirge.[1]

Among the prominent accompaniments of ancient Hebrew mourning for the dead, the most notable were the rending of garments (2 Sam. iii. 31), and the casting of dust or ashes on the head (Josh. vii. 6; 2 Sam. i. 2), and the wearing of sackcloth, walking bareheaded or barefoot (Ezek. xxiv. 17; 2 Sam. xv. 30). Among the more extravagant and heathenish practices may be mentioned the mutilations of the body, the shaving of the hair, and the cropping of the beard (Jer. xvi. 6, xli. 5, xlvii. 5; Isa. xxii. 12; Mic. i. 16). Fasting was ordained for seven days after the death of Saul (1 Sam. xxxi. 13), closed each day after sunset by a feast (Hos. ix. 4; 2 Sam. iii. 35; Jer. xvi. 7 foll.; Ezek. xxiv. 17, 22). This practice, however, should be connected with the tradition of offerings to the dead, to which we find a reference in Deuteronomy xxvi. 14. And the burning of spices, which in later times became customary in honour of distinguished persons (Jer. xxxiv. 5; 2 Chron. xvi. 14), is to be ascribed to a like origin.

---

[1] Comp. Joseph., *Wars of the Jews*, iii. 9, 5, and the closing passage of the 'Descent of Ishtar to Hades.'

CHAPTER III

SOCIAL AND POLITICAL ORGANIZATION

27. In the most primitive forms of human society **the clan** rather than **the family** appears to have been the basis upon which the life of the community rested. In fact, as the late Professor Robertson Smith has shown us, kinship or clan membership seems to be an older thing than family life. But whatever may be said of the earliest conditions of Semitic society, it is quite certain that the social life of the Old Testament regards the family (or 'house') as a distinct entity, and the father of the family or house is regarded as the master of his wife, children, and slaves. As the sons married and begat children, the family became extended into a larger household group, of which the father of the original family was the 'head' (1 Chron. v. 15), and possessed the right of making the customary offerings on behalf of the members of the household (Job i. 5), and also of settling disputes. These different 'household groups' or 'houses of fathers' (Exod. xii. 3) constituted a clan. But the word is sometimes used apparently in an extended sense, so as to mean a 'clan' or 'tribe' (Num. iii. 24, 30, xvii. 2; Josh xxii. 14).

Religion was in ancient times the cement which

held society together. What was true of early Greek and Roman national life equally applies to that of the ancient Hebrew. The life of the clan was sustained and its members welded together into a social unity by the *sacra*, or religious rites of sacrifice practised by its members at certain seasons (as New Moon or annual festival). The sacrifice was offered to the Lord of the land and Giver of earthly good, and the flesh was eaten by the participating members, who thereby renewed the covenant bond that united them to their Lord and God, and also bound them to one another. Another link of connection which bound the tribe or clan together was the grave of a common ancestor, which was usually marked by a tree (Gen. xxxv. 20; Josh. xxiv. 32; Gen. xii. 6; xxv. 10; Deut. xi. 30). A clan might easily grow by additions from without, such as slaves who had won their freedom, runaway slaves who settled in the territory of the clan, and resident foreigners (*gērim*) who became absorbed into the community. On the other hand, various accidents, as war or famine, might cause a large clan or tribe to split up into different clans or tribes.

The distinction between the clan and the tribe is not always clearly marked. Thus the small tribe of Dan is called a 'clan' (Judg. xviii. 11). But, according to ordinary usage, a group of clans made up a tribe (*shēbhet*), and a group of tribes constituted a people or nation.

Among the Arabs at the head of the clan stands the *shaich*. Though he does not actually command, but only advise, his weight in the counsels of the community is considerable. He leads the clan in war, and conducts the negotiations for peace. But his authority is limited, and he cannot take a decisive and important step without consulting the chief men of his clan or tribe. These chief men, constituting the *divan* of the shaich, correspond closely to the 'elders' of the ancient Hebrew commonwealth.

The growth of agricultural life, and the greater interests it involved, together with the need of common defence, tended to weld the different clans together. Under these circumstances, and mainly under the stress of war, a group of clans or tribes would rally round a 'judge' (*shôphet* or *katzîn*) (Judg. xi. 6). His position for the time would be supreme over the 'princes' or 'elders' in each clan. The desperate life and death struggle of the central tribes against the Philistines ultimately united them under Saul. Subsequently, under the leadership of David, Judah joined the confederation.

In this way monarchy gradually arose, for the distinction between the position of Gideon and that of Saul is not a great one. Like the 'judge,' the king was a military leader, and like the judge, he decided suits between individuals at the gate. Comp. 2 Samuel xiv.; xv. 2–4; 1 Kings iii. 16 foll. Moreover the Hebrew kings resembled those of Assyria in possessing the highest priestly functions. As such they were solemnly anointed, and it is from this tradition the conception of the 'Messiah' or 'the Anointed One' (Christ) originated (1 Sam. x. 1, xvi. 1, 13, xxiv. 10; 2 Sam. i. 14, xix. 21; 2 Kings ix. 1, 3). Consequently the king performed sacrifice as the people's representative before God (1 Sam. xiii. 9, xiv. 34; 2 Sam. vi. 13, 17). David wore the priest's linen ephod, while in 1 Kings viii. 14 we read that Solomon, at the opening of his temple, bestowed a solemn blessing on the people (comp. 2 Sam. vi. 18). Also the king had the power of appointing priests. David appears to have appointed his own sons (2 Sam. viii. 18). Indeed, the power of royalty and the number of its subordinates, as might be expected, considerably increased under David and Solomon. These are mentioned in 2 Samuel viii. 16–18. First among them was the *chief commander* over the host. Next came the '*recorder*' (or *chronicler*'), whose function was not only to keep the state records, but, as chief adviser of the king or prime minister, to '*remind*' him of all necessary facts, and suggest the best course to be pursued (2 Kings xviii. 18, 37; Isa. xxxvi. 3, 22; 2 Chron. xxxiv. 8). Also the *state secretary* ('scribe') conducted the royal correspondence with officials and foreign princes. The *commander of the king's body guard*, called 'mighty men' or 'Cherethites and Pelethites' (Cretans and Philistines). As the organization of the kingdom developed in the reign of Solomon and his successors, other offices were created. Among these should be noticed the *overseer of the burdens* or 'taskmaster'; the *minister of the household* or palace (Isa. xxii. 15; xxxvi. 3, 22), the 'servant of the king' (2 Kings xxii. 12), a special office of which nothing definite can be ascertained, except that he probably belonged to the court or harem. Among the subordinate officials there were *prefects* over the thirteen provinces; the *cupbearer* (1 Kings x. 5); the *overseer of the king's wardrobe* ('over the vestry,' 2 Kings x. 22); twelve *overseers of the royal treasure*, and, lastly, *chamberlains*.

The powers exercised by the king became at the close of Solomon's reign of a very oppressive character, and in the fluid condition of Hebrew politics caused by the loose cohesion of the tribes they ultimately destroyed the unity of Israel. The slaughter of the priests of Nob in the days of Saul, David's conduct towards Uriah, his arbitrary treatment of Joab, and the severe burdens of taxation imposed on the people by Solomon in order to minister to his love of splendour and luxury, exhibit a steady growth in the extent and use of royal prerogatives.

The judicial murder of Naboth is a further example of the excessive lengths to which the arbitrary power of the monarch extended during the dynasty of Omri. The supreme power wielded by the king in the administration of justice as *shôphet* doubtless came to overshadow that which was exercised by the heads of clans. It is certain, however, that these princes (*sarîm*) or 'elders' of the town community (which gradually displaced the ancient clan), exercised their judicial functions in quite as oppressive and corrupt a manner as their royal master did. The prophets of the eighth and seventh centuries are full of denunciations of their cruel injustice to the poor and their acceptance of bribes (Isa. i. 23, v. 7, 22 foll.; Mic. iii. 11, vii. 3, etc.).

Our information is defective respecting the *revenues* by which the royal state was maintained. In the time of Saul they probably consisted of a portion of the spoil (2 Sam. viii. 11, xii. 30), and the gifts of foreign princes and others who offered him homage or sought his protection. In the time of David royalty depended not only on these sources of revenue, but also on the tribute of conquered races. Nowack considers that the numbering of the people under David was connected not only with the arrangements for military service, but also for national taxation. This we know to have been the object of the division of territory under Solomon into thirteen districts (1 Kings iv. 7, not twelve, as Stade and Nowack have shown). From Amos vii. 1 we learn that a kind of firstfruits from pasture called 'king's mowings' fell to the share of the monarch, for the support of his war horses, as we may gather from 1 Kings xviii. 5. Special contributions were sometimes levied by the king to meet special emergencies, as the payment of a victorious foe (2 Kings xv. 20, xxiii. 35). After the exile we find at first twelve men or elders standing at the head of the young Jewish community, the chief place among them being held by Joshua and Zerubbabel (Ezra ii. and Neh. vii.). These twelve men represented the nation in all transactions with the Persian government. Whatever hopes may have gathered round Zerubbabel as a descendant of the line of David (Zech. vi. 9 foll.), it was the *High Priest* Joshua who represented the supreme power of the future, destined to absorb into itself the privileges and functions of the pre-exilian Hebrew king. In the Greek period the high priest is the head of the nation, and in the days of the Maccabees the line of Asmonæan priest-princes was inaugurated. The high priest was the president of a supreme court of justice called the *Sanhedrin*, which sat in Jerusalem and exercised its functions over Judæa. To this supreme court belonged the scribes, elders, and priestly nobility, and all cases which were not reserved for the decision of the *procurator*, or did not come before the local courts, were examined by this highest tribunal. Its origin cannot be traced earlier than the Greek period.

APPENDIX

A.—Money.

1. *Silver.*		£	s.	d.
1 Talent	=	412	10	0
1 Maneh	=	6	17	6

($=\frac{1}{60}$th of a Talent).

		£	s.	d.
1 Shekel	=	0	2	9

($=\frac{1}{50}$th of a Maneh).

2. *Gold.*		£	s.	d.
1 Talent	=	6187	10	0
1 Maneh	=	103	2	6
1 Shekel	=	2	1	3

During the Greek and Roman periods the following coinage was current:—

		£	s.	d.
Talent . . .	=	240	0	0
Mina . . .	=	4	0	0

($=\frac{1}{60}$ Talent).

		£	s.	d.
Stater or Tetradrachm .	=	0	2	8

($\frac{1}{30}$th of Mina).

		£	s.	d.
Didrachm .	=	0	1	4

		d.
Denarius or Drachma	=	8
Assarion or As . .	=	$\frac{1}{2}$

('Penny').

		d.
Quadrans ('Farthing')	=	$\frac{1}{8}$
Lepton or 'Mite' .	=	$\frac{1}{16}$

B.—Weights.

1 Talent = about 160 lbs.
1 Maneh (Mina) = 2 lbs. 8 ozs. (Troy).
1 Shekel = 10 dwts. 14 grs. (nearly).
1 Bekah = 5 ,, 7 ,, ,,
1 Gerah = 13 ,, ,,

APPENDIX

C.—MEASURES OF CAPACITY AND LENGTH.

1 Homer = 80 gallons.
1 Lethech = 40 gallons.
 (= ½ Homer.)
1 Ephah or Bath = 8 gallons.
 (= 1/10 Homer.)
1 Seah = 2⅔ gallons.
1 Hin = 1⅓ gallons.
1 Omer = 6 pints.
1 Cab (= ⅓ Hin) = 3½ pints.
1 Log = ⅞ pint.

1 Reed = 9 feet.
1 Cubit = 1 foot 6 inches.
 (= ⅙ Reed.)
1 Span = 9 inches.
 (= ½ Cubit.)
1 Palm = 3 inches.
 (= ⅓ Span.)
1 Digit = ¾ inch.

D.—JEWISH CALENDAR.

The most ancient Hebrew and Semitic Calendar was purely agricultural, as the names *Abib* (ear of corn), *Ziv* (blossom), *Bûl* (fruit), and *Ethanim* (flowing brooks) clearly indicate. The last two names of months occur also on Phœnician or Canaanite inscriptions, and it is evident that these names, which were employed by pre-exilian Israel, were of Canaanite origin. The Feast of Tabernacles or Ingathering thus came at the 'end of the year' (Exod. xxiii. 16, xxxiv. 22), and the beginning of the new year was in October. During and after the exile a change was introduced through Babylonian influence. The names of the months were different since they were borrowed from the Babylonians. Cuneiform research has confirmed Rabbinic tradition by demonstrating that all the names of months, excepting those mentioned above, are Babylonian (viz., Nisan, Iyyar, Sivan, etc.). The year now commenced with Nisan or Abib, and not with Tishri. This new calendar became identified with the *Ecclesiastical Year*, while the old Canaanite Calendar is preserved in what is called the *Civil Year*. As the months were strictly lunar, the year of 12 months consisted of 354 days, and in order to make up the extra 11 days of the solar year (of 365 days), an intercalary month, Veadar, was necessary. The following list of Hebrew months will be found useful :—

Abib or *Nisan* (March–April).
  1st. Beginning of the Sacred Year. New Moon.
  14th. *Preparation for Passover.* In the evening of this day the *Paschal meal* was eaten.
  15th. Holy Convocation and Sabbath. Week of *Unleavened Bread* begins.

Iyyar (or *Ziv*) (April–May).

Sivan (May–June).
  6th and 7th. *Pentecost* or Feast of Weeks (called in Book of the Covenant 'Feast of Harvest'), being seven weeks from the days of 'Unleavened Bread.'

Tammuz (June–July).

Ab (July–August).

Elul (August–September).
  15th–22nd. *Feast of Tabernacles* or *Booths.*
  21st. *Feast of Branches* or *Palms.*

Tishri (September–October) or *Ethanim.*
  1st. New Moon or *New Year's Day* (*beginning of the Civil Year*). Feast of Trumpets.
  10th. *Day of Atonement.*
  16th. Offering of Omer, or first sheaf.
  21st. Holy Convocation.

Marchesvan or *Bûl* (October–November).

Kislev (November–December).
  25th. *Chanuccah* or *Feast of Dedication.*

Tebeth (December–January).

Shebat (January–February).

Adar (February–March).
  13th. *Fast of Esther.*
  14th and 15th. *Feast of Purim.*

Veadar (intercalary month).

E. SACRIFICES.

IN the early nomadic stage of Israel's life, the *bloody* offering was the prevailing type of sacrifice at the altar. Its hoary antiquity gave it a certain superiority above every other. In Genesis iv. Cain and the Cainite race represent the growth of civilization, while Abel is the representative of simple nomadic life. In those early days sacrifice was a meal which bound the participating worshippers together around the deity who was worshipped, and the blood of the slaughtered victim was sprinkled or smeared on the upright stone symbol. The slaughtered lamb or ox would be the ordinary form of offering, and was called *zebach*. Of this the worshippers partook.

But other kinds of food came in early times to be employed in the sacrificial meal. And these naturally came to be more prominent as agricultural life increased, and so rendered the use of oil and flour more common in food. Thus the *unleavened barley-cakes* (*mazzôth*), eaten at the annual Easter festival, were an ordinary article of diet in a primitive Hebrew household; but it obviously presupposes the beginnings of agriculture, and a higher stage of civilization than the sacrifice of a lamb. The same remark obviously applies to the use of *oil* in sacrificial offerings (Gen. xxviii. 18). In fact the ritual system of the Hebrew codes, presupposed to a certain extent in the historical books and prophets, clearly reveals the developed agricultural life of the people. *Milk* is curiously not an ingredient of offerings, but we read on special occasions of *water-offerings* (1 Sam. vii. 6; 2 Sam. xxiii. 16; comp. 1 Kings xviii. 33–35; Josh. ix. 27). Reference has already been made to the *raisin-cakes* (*ashîshah*) employed in offerings (Hos. iii. 1; 2 Sam. vi. 9). Jeremiah (vii. 18) also refers to the cakes or wafers made from dough (*kawwân*) for Ashtoreth, queen of heaven. This is illustrated from an interesting Phœnician inscription discovered in Cyprus, which contains a list of expenses for the month *Ethanim*: 'For the architects who have built the temple of Ashtoreth, for each house . . . for two sacrifices . . for two bakers who have baked the cakes for the holy Queen.'

Primitive antiquity reveals the grim fact of *human sacrifice* This prevailed extensively in the early dawn of human civilization. Of this we find constant traces, not only in Greek and Roman antiquity (Iphigeneia and Marcus Curtius), but in the Old Testament itself. The most notable examples are to be found in the revolting cult of Moab and Ammon. In the case of the Moabites, who worshipped Chemosh, we have the terrible example of the sacrifice of the king's eldest son, recorded in 2 Kings iii. 27, while the horrible rites of Molech, god of Ammon, were carried on in the Valley of Hinnom (comp. Jer. vii. 31; 2 Kings xxiii. 10, 13; Deut. xii. 31; Ezek. xvi. 20, 21,

xxiii. 37 ; 2 Chron. xxviii. 3). These 'abominations of the children of Ammon' were strictly forbidden in the Deuteronomic legislation. Among the primitive Hebrews prisoners taken in war were too often dedicated to destruction (*chérem*), such acts being regarded as invested with sanctity (Josh. viii. 26 ; x. 28, 37, xi. 21 ; 1 Sam. xv. 3 foll.). These were the ordinary and almost inseparable accompaniments of war. For war in ancient times had a sacred character, and was initiated by special sacrifices, which welded together the participating tribes or clans by a close covenant bond (1 Sam. xi. 7 foll.; 1 Kings i. 9). From this slaughter of enemies we must separate such special and peculiar acts as the sacrifice of the King of Moab's eldest son, and the surrender of Michal's sons to be slaughtered by the Gibeonites. These were extraordinary piacular sacrifices intended to appease Divine wrath and avert some special evil. So to the storm-tossed heroes returning from Troy the oracle declared *sanguine placabis ventos et virgine cæsa*.

In bright contrast with these were the ordinary genial rites of sacrifice practised by the clan at the new moon, or annual festival (1 Sam. ix. 12 foll., xx. 6). In course of time a distinction was made between the earlier *bloody* offerings and the *vegetable*, or *meal offerings*. The first was called by the general name of *zebach*, or *shelem*, or the two names were combined into one expression. *Shelem* is best rendered by '*peace-offering*,' since it expressed the state of friendship or communion between the worshipper and his God. A peace-offering might be presented in discharge of a vow, and a certain portion consumed by the worshipper at his own home instead of in assembled concourse. But this practice grew up later, viz., after the suppression of the local sanctuaries (comp. Prov. vii. 14).

The vegetable, or 'meal-offerings' (a better phrase than the 'meat-offerings' of the A.V.) were of the nature of a gift, and were, therefore, called by the special name of *minchah*, 'gift,' or 'present.' At first this term was used for any offering, and accordingly is applied by the ancient writer of Genesis iv. alike to the sacrifice of Abel and of Cain. But in later times it was appropriated to the vegetable or meal-offerings only, and it is the word rendered 'meal-offering' in the Revised Version. This offering expressed the idea of gift, whereas the bloody offering expressed that of communion between God and the worshipper.

There was yet another form of sacrifice which expressed the idea of gift still more strongly as an offering *wholly* presented to God, viz., the *whole burnt-offering*, called in Hebrew *'ôlah*, or *kalîl*, terms frequently combined (1 Sam. vii. 9; Deut. xiii. 16). The latter word occurs more often in Phœnician inscriptions. The fundamental conception of the *'ôlah* was self-dedication, and it found expression in 'sending up to Jehovah, in the form of smoke,' the victim presented.

The idea and ritual of *sin-offerings* are probably more ancient than some writers are disposed to think. Doubtless the ethical conception of sin was one of gradual growth, stimulated by the teachings of the prophets, who constantly inculcated the necessity of righteousness in conduct as the only basis of man's satisfactory relationship to God. This circle of ideas became attached to the Jewish sacrificial system, and found its fullest expression in the ethical sense of guilt involved in the impressive ceremonial of the great Day of Atonement. This conception of sin-offering for human guilt, with the ideas of substitution and mediation which are involved, are of special value to all disciples of Christ. For they interpret Christ's mediatorial work as High Priest and the sacrifice offered in His death (Heb. ix. 11, 26).

www.ingramcontent.com/pod-product-compliance
Lightning Source LLC
Chambersburg PA
CBHW030306170426
43202CB00009B/893